WITH K

Britain Beyond Europe

Britain
Beyond Europe

Bill Jamieson

Duckworth

First published in 1994 by
Gerald Duckworth & Co. Ltd.
The Old Piano Factory
48 Hoxton Square, London N1 6PB
Tel: 071 729 5986
Fax: 071 729 0015

A catalogue record for this book is available
from the British Library

ISBN 0 7156 2611 6

Typeset by Ray Davies
Printed in Great Britain by
Biddles Ltd., Guildford & King's Lynn

BUSINESS

Contents

To Elaine and Alastair and Iain and Susan

Foreword
by Stephen Hill

There is not a single person in Britain who would disagree with the proposition that the nation has suffered a continuous decline in varying hues and degrees in the half-century since the Second World War. It was in recognition of this stark fact that John Major launched his 'Back to Basics' programme in October 1993. Yet within months this glib initiative had unwittingly become the surrogate agent of bourgeois morality, and all for want of clear definition.

This timely book by Bill Jamieson takes a much closer look at the causes of our decline, for solutions can only be revealed by proper diagnosis of our present national syndromes. The subject is at once complicated and even bizarre. A nation that fifty years ago received the two largest enemy capitulations in Europe and destroyed the Japanese army in Burma is now told that it only has any future at all inside a bureaucratic political union forged by its former vanquished enemy and vanquished ally, while many sectors of its industry depend increasingly on Japanese and German involvement for survival.

It is extraordinary that this should be so. The English language pervades the world as it fast becomes the first truly global language. Britain's overseas investments, mainly in the English-speaking world, are second to none. Three of the world's top ten corporations are British. In relation to her one-and-a-half per cent of world population, British scientists have won around a quarter of the Nobel prizes for science. And yet when John Major signed the Maastricht Treaty in 1993, Britain signed away as yet unknown powers over her very own future to eleven non-English-speaking nations across the Channel.

How did a nation, with such a startling record of success in so many fields, and in the oh-so-recent past, come to such an abject view of its own capacity for self-determination and its position in the world? Jamieson's analysis is succinct: if our leaders and their advisers cannot drive, deflect or exploit events from the firm standpoint of the principle of the sovereignty of the nation state, then events will certainly drive, deflect and expose them. Britain's problems derive not from an excess of overt failings of those that are led, but by the seemingly endless capacity of our leaders to think small and sell the line of least resistance. This creeping destruction has now reached the point where our once-mighty institutions now themselves seem frail and ready to totter for lack of clear leadership.

Since 1979 the Conservative and Unionist Party has been in continuous power. Conservatism used to mean the retention of those institutions and practices that were plainly good and useful, combined with an almost sceptical approach on most occasions to the new-fangled and untested, which was then accepted, if at all, only slowly and cautiously. The sorry state of the nation at the end of the 1970s called for a radical approach in many fields, from industrial relations to the size of the public sector, and Britain's first woman Prime Minister had the policies and the conviction to meet the pressing need. Unfortunately, her reforming zeal was eventually perceived to have got ahead of itself and her party's support during her third term of office. Nevertheless, important sectors such as education, local government and industrial investment were either still in disarray or substantially overlooked.

These specific failings, however, were as nothing compared to the general dismay experienced by the public at large in the early 1990s, as they gazed in bewilderment at the irreversible closure of famous regiments, squadrons, naval dockyards, coalmines, fishing fleets, along with industries as diverse as small- and medium-bore steel tubes to telecommunications equipment manufacturing, and centuries-old hospitals that are the envy of the world – while all the while the social security budget rose inexorably as unemployment passed the 3,000,000 mark. As a sure reflection of the impoverished condition of our island race, the Royal Navy was meanwhile reduced to just thirty-five surface ships of the line. Our leaders, it seems, have confused government of the people with management of a national profit and loss account, as they carelessly exchange excellence for so-called efficiency.

Then, in 1993, the *Conservative* government signed, without so much as a by-your-leave from the great British public, a treaty which will soon hand over to foreign powers and institutions final sovereignty over our law, economy and foreign policy in exchange for a vague notion called 'subsidiarity' – unless an irreducible core of clear-thinking Euro-sceptics wins the battle of ideas and the war. It was almost inevitable that this same government would then within months cede to the bomb and the bullet and gamble the Union itself, in exchange for a glimmer of hope for peace in Ulster. The people of Ulster, it seems, may determine their future sovereignty, while those on the mainland are denied a referendum on a substantially equivalent issue – such are the illogicalities inherent in this untested political concept. For subsidiarity, it seems, has different meanings, depending on whether you are looking across the Channel or the Irish Sea.

While democracy yields to terrorism, the government allows an excessive concentration of media power that now seems to wield more influence than the great institutions of state themselves. Democracy in Britain is now itself under serious threat, not just from the excesses of a partisan press, but from the marginalisation of champions of opposing views, the stifling of debate on issues by threats, and the deliberate suppression of documents – not least the Maastricht Treaty itself, which was withheld from the public until after the April 1992 election. Meanwhile the dysfunctional opposition parties lamely endorse 'conservative' policies, waiting for a socialist breeze from the continent to fill their idly flapping sails with Monetary Union and the Social Chapter.

This is the Conservative party's dilemma, as the only effective opposition comes from its own backbenches and even threatens, ultimately, to split this most enduring of political parties. This is because the Conservative Europhiles have failed to achieve any clear endorsement from their own electorate. Public opinion might therefore favour a split so that the majority of the people in the country could once again be enfranchised on this most crucial issue. It is ironic, and possibly tragic, that the left wing of the party which invokes the 'One Nation' dictum should now be repudiating that famous observation of Disraeli: 'The Tory Party is a national party or it is nothing.'

The right wing senses the advance of a new-look international socialist theory that believes in the twin follies of monetary union across a disparate continent of ever-increasing social security. Now regional social cohesion grants are to be doled out by a centralist and constructivist folly – the EU – in order to subsume our nationhood in the name of a lasting European peace, as though the dreaming rationalists of 1822 had been freshly recycled in a strangely coincidental and cultish metempsychosis. The right wing looks on in disbelief as it begins to detect an arithmetical ratio between the dissolution of our armed defences, coupled with the relentless advance of domestic crime, and the increasing loss of sovereignty of our established church, constitutional monarchy and democratic parliament.

Apart from a brief spell in the 1980s when the successful management of events and self-generated achievements temporarily gave our island nation the feeling of natural greatness once again, our leaders in too many fields have besmirched the good name of patriotism, conflating it with xenophobia, nationalism and other absurd epithets. All too often they have told us why we cannot achieve what we were poised to accomplish anyway, given only the springboard of clear and confident leadership. Our current leaders, meanwhile, can only point to the state of the rest of the world and claim that our problems are the product of a global phenomenon. This apology is false, and for reasons that are not necessarily obvious, as Jamieson carefully demonstrates in his analysis of the long post-war decline. For as Shakespeare advised us concerning that most basic of all basics, in words that meant what he said and said what he meant, 'Tis in ourselves that we are thus, or thus'.

London
February 1994

Acknowledgments

On the economics chapters I am indebted to Michael Howell, global strategist at Baring Securities, and his assistant Angela Cozzini: their research on cross-border equity flows and emerging markets investment is now pre-eminent in London; and to Bill Martin, chief UK economist of UBS for his comments and advice on the chapters on the UK economy. I thank also Sir Chips Keswick of Hambros Bank; Roger Bootle, head of UK economics and Alison Cottrell, European markets analyst at Midland Global Markets; John Jay, City Editor of the *Sunday Telegraph*, and the press officers at the Treasury, Bank of England and Department of Trade and Industry for their help.

One of the keenest legal minds on the Maastricht Treaty has been that of Martin Howe, and I am indebted to him for his guidance both on the Treaty and the European Court of Justice. On the political front, I owe much to William Cash MP for his briefings and his comments on the political chapters; to Dr Martin Holmes, co-chairman of the Bruges Group; to Brian Kingham, former Bruges Group Treasurer; and Sir Tom Arnold MP.

I am particularly appreciative of the encouragement of Lindsay Jenkins, whose support in the early stages was invaluable, and her comments on the early drafts, constructive and intelligent, as always; and to Stephen Hill and Colin Haycraft at Duckworth.

Most of all, I am indebted to Lord Harris of High Cross for his help on the later drafts. He has been an inspiration, not only on this project but on my economic thinking over many years, and I owe a very special acknowledgment.

The day is coming, if it has not already come, when the question of the balance of power cannot be confined to Europe alone ... England, though she is bound to Europe by tradition, by affection, by great similarity of habits, and all those ties which time alone can create and consecrate, is not a mere Power of the old world. Her geographical position, her laws, her language and religion, connect her as much with the New World as with the old. And although she has occupied an eminent ... position among European nations for ages, still, if ever Europe by her shortsightedness falls into an inferior and exhausted state, for England there will remain an illustrious future. We are bound to communities of the New World and those great states which our own planting and colonising energies have created, by ties and interests which will sustain our power and enable us to play as great a part in the times yet to come as we do in these days and we have done in the past. ... I say it is for Europe and not for England, that my heart sinks.

Benjamin Disraeli, 1859

1

The Last Great Coup

We persist in regarding ourselves as a Great Power, capable of everything and only temporarily handicapped by economic difficulties. We are not a great power and never will be again. We are a great nation, but if we continue to behave like a Great Power we shall soon cease to be a great nation.

Sir Henry Tizard, Chief Adviser to the
Ministry of Defence, 1950

The British have formed the habit of praising their institutions, which are sometimes inept, and of ignoring the character of their race, which is often superb. In the end they will be in danger of losing their character and being left with their institutions, a result disastrous indeed.

Lord Radcliffe, Reith Lecture, December 1951

For everyone born in Britain since 1945, the notion of national decline has come to be accepted as a fact of life. Her people have adapted to it as a natural condition of being British, an inevitable and unrelenting loss of place and purpose. Here was a remnant inheritance, a folk memory of Empire repressed by guilt and a sense of there being no other destiny left to play out other than integration as reluctant Europeans.

The hope of the British political and business elite was that integration with Europe would mitigate, if not arrest, such a decline by substituting a new sense of purpose and place for the fading impulse of the old. No such renewal has arisen. Europe, with its over-regulated, uncompetitive welfare economies, plunged into a recession deeper and more prolonged than any in the Anglo-Saxon world. It accelerated her decline in world markets and loss of importance in the global economy, adding to her crisis of identity. The loss of Britain's place in the world, the faltering purpose, the impoverishment of spirit at home and the dissolution of national consciousness and self-esteem have proceeded to a degree unimaginable to our parents and grandparents.

So pervasive has been the change in culture, institutions and outlook that there is no serious writer in Britain today who does not hesitate before applying the word 'nation' to Britain. The island that dissolved its empire has been brought, by a combination of domestic failure and external loss of will, to a final crisis, not of power but of definition.

Yet by other measures there has been a benign and liberal improvement. Living standards, average incomes and personal wealth are indisputably higher than in the immediate post-war years. Consumer choice, health care, housing standards, availability of education, working conditions, amenities and social services have risen to a degree inconceivable to the Beveridge generation. Spending on social security alone has risen almost eightfold in real terms since 1949.

Britain's economy was the first in the European Community to show recovery. Britain entered 1994 with the lowest inflation for 26 years, low interest rates and falling unemployment. But at the heart of this recovery there was a vacuum of conviction and vision. What was recovery to be for?

Despite the maintenance of a sophisticated welfare dispensary and evidence of a consumer-spending upturn, the nation that prime minister John Major wanted to be 'at ease with itself' was ever more beaten down by inner-city decay, violence, crime, economic enfeeblement and a collapse of spirit and ideas. What was worrying in all of this was not the slide in confidence *per se* but that it had permeated deep into that which had protected Britain in the past – her culture and her institutions.

In a poll published in 1993, before John Major's 'back to basics' call was to founder in confusion and scandal, more than a third of the population could not think of a single thing about Britain to be proud of and nearly half said that they would emigrate if they could. Pride in Britain and confidence in her institutions had sunk to rock-bottom.

The pervasive sense of a civic deconstruction stemmed from a loss of confidence and esteem in almost every area of British life. A Gallup survey at the end of 1993 found that 86 per cent of respondents believed that moral standards had deteriorated, and 74 per cent said that educational standards had fallen. This verdict was founded not just on the bald statistics of crime – notifiable offences up 60 per cent in the four years to 1992 to a record 5.5 million – but on a loss of faith in the ability of the authorities to improve matters. When Sir Henry Tizard warned that Britain might cease to be a great nation, he could not have conceived of how great would be the loss of the unifying sensibility of nationhood that has been a salient feature of the past thirty years.

Such is the background to a 'great nation' whose morale, purpose and definition has come into question, and whose government formally signalled, over the heads of the people of Ulster, Britain had 'no selfish economic or strategic interest' in their remaining part of the United Kingdom, an observation that caused many to wonder to what other parts of Britain this fateful phrase might not in time come to apply.

Britain was been brought to believe that there is no longer an indigenous solution; that the game of island is truly up. There have been many causes. This book is concerned with three in particular. First has been the collapse of confidence suffered by the British Establishment and the political class, traceable to the aftermath of Suez, which it has transmitted to every section of the population. Starting from that breakdown, the elite effectively lost sight of Britain's unique culture and her institutions and the will to defend them. This loss of respect for the sovereignty of her institutions, and the sovereignty of the British people of which they were the supreme expression, has been the prime error of this generation. Second has been our failure to order the concerns of the British state around the fundamental requirement of viability, both on the public finances and on the external trading account.

And third has been the rise of welfarism and the dependency culture, predicated on the notion that the prime function of the state is to act as a welfare dispensary through one of the most sophisticated and costly benefit systems in the industrialised world. This dispensary, which has expanded far beyond the ambitions of its founder William Beveridge, has grown to be the single largest function and expense of the British state. It has done so by default. It became the substitute *raison d'être* of the state over a period when Britain was in imperial and economic retreat. Welfare expansion was the means by which the political class sustained itself in office. Spending soared from 4.7 per cent of GDP in 1950 to more than 12 per cent, swollen by the demands of a poorly educated and under-skilled multi-ethnic underclass in the inner cities. Welfare spending, in which the main political parties sought to outbid and out-provide each other, became the post-war equivalent of *Dreadnought* and the Navy Race. The expansion of welfare proceeded in direct counter-point to the decline in Britain's share of world trade in manufactures – from 25 per cent in 1950 to 6 per cent now – and a commensurate decline in Britain's productive base.

And it is this combination, of self-fuelling welfare expansion and a declining productive base that led, first, to a soaring budget deficit and to the current programme of £30 billion of tax increases over three years – the biggest revenue-exercise ever undertaken by a British government. That it was ushered in by an administration pledged to low taxation only added to the mood of weary cynicism and to a further loss of purpose, cohesion and pride.

Yet this was subsidiary to a greater error: the pursuit of continental integration and the loss of economic and political sovereignty. Here is a continuum along which the Maastricht Treaty was less a culmination than an intermediate step. Yet Maastricht, with all its numbing language and baffling protocols, its grinding legalistic wheels and ratchets, was a moment of truth for Britain, much more than the Treaty of Accession and the Single European Act. However much it was presented as an opportunity to be 'right at the heart of Europe', yet with earnest assurances that it had no substantive constitutional implications it was impossible to hide the loss of control involved in a Treaty whose full title deserved greater prominence than it got: the Treaty on European Union.

For Maastricht to be accepted, its apologists played to a long-nurtured mood of fatalism that further integration with Europe was inevitable. It was not in Maastricht itself, but in the resignation and inertia required for its acceptance, the political equivalent of metal fatigue, that can be traced the final eclipse of the British state. Not by foreign imposition but by voluntary acquiescence we would abandon the mind-set of island. We would be something different, something else. We would not be Britain. We would be Benelux West.

From Empire to Benelux West: for Britain to have been held together on this road, to have been willingly talked out of her world outlook and inheritance, has been a colossal feat of the Establishment, its last great coup. It succeeded in convincing a nation of 57 million people that what it first presented as membership of a market, participation in which would help British commerce and trade, was in fact a political programme with the ultimate goal of monetary and political union.

For the coup to succeed not only did its aims have to be disguised. A calculated assault had to be made on the remaining pockets of national self-confidence. At the heart of the case for British integration with Europe was a view, espoused at the highest levels of the City, the Foreign Office and the Treasury, that Britain was effectively incapable of survival as an independent economic and sovereign state.

According to those who opposed entry, Britain acceded to integration with Europe in a fit of national forgetfulness, a mystical lapse of concentration. Were the British bewitched or hypnotised? Was it a conscious act or a collective sleep-walk? The truth is surely more harsh. Far from 'sleep-walking' into Europe, Britain succumbed to a European destiny fully conscious and only after the most extensive debate, referendum and repeated affirmation by Parliament. Britain, or more accurately its political class, entered into a Faustian pact: it saw in Europe a means of breaking free from chronic balance of payments and domestic policy constraints that had dogged Britain since the early 1960s. For that economic advantage and the political rewards it would bring, successive governments were prepared to cede national sovereignty.

Economic benefit was the myth at the heart of Europe and the surprise in retrospect was not so much that this myth came to prevail as that it cast its legitimising spell for so long. For the political class the continental option, however much the compromise of sovereignty entailed, was preferable to the radical domestic re-arrangement that would otherwise have been necessary to tackle the economy. To propound the myth of economic benefit through membership of the EC it was necessary to portray all alternatives to it as flawed, or costly or unworkable. Thus we were constantly told that Britain could not survive outside Europe. We were continually reminded of our smallness and our inadequacy; warned that there was no alternative but 'bankruptcy'. For a generation the British political elite did not lift a hand to spare the people from a consciousness of failure. On the contrary, every occasion was used to batter that consciousness into us. The less confidence Britain had in herself, the more she looked to Benelux West. We were told, of course, that we would still be Britain, in that triumph of shadow over substance that John Major conjured up, of Sunday church and village cricket and warm beer. Only the endless twilight of decline and failure would be over. By a collective metamorphosis, that switch from British to European consciousness, we would be free of the sickly, terminal condition of Britishness. If only we ceased to be an island, we would be cured.

Through the ratification of the Treaty on European Union the British were encouraged to see themselves no longer as citizens of a distinct and separate country but as part of a wider community. Once convergence is complete, the only unifying experience will be of living under the administrative jurisdiction of the United Kingdom. That a common administrative zone no more makes for 'nation' than a building with its walls knocked out makes for a home is the conclusion that the continentalised British were encouraged to draw. That they found this difficult and unsettling should come as no surprise. For the continental countries, where the fact of continent has been a basic determinant of outlook, it may still feel, as they move towards union, that a branch of the tree of national experience is being sawn off. But for Britain to lose the mind-set of island is a loss of an altogether different quality: it is to saw off not a branch but the very trunk of her history and experience.

What was once a broadly shared set of institutions, values and symbols regarded with pride is assigned to a past with which large sections of the population neither identify nor are encouraged to seek identification. Perhaps it is no cause for wonder, still less for concern, than in 1993 10 per cent of 17-year-olds could no longer identify the United Kingdom on a map. Less measurable but as disconcerting is the loss of uniqueness, the relentless theft of myth and memory, like lead being stripped off a church roof. The British are losing sight of who they are, to become the people they have never been, the residents of an all-too-present Erewhon.

Meanwhile Parliament was assured that the lofty prose of the Treaty of Maastricht's preamble had no real meaning; that it was language with no substance, rhetoric only, 'it didn't really mean what it said'. Nothing more caught the last redoubt of the Establishment than the attempt to present the Treaty on Euro-

pean Union as other than what it was. This loss of understanding of fundamental national interest has extended right
across the administrative elite and the political class. Voters
had no real say in the Single European Act, economic convergence, the ERM or Maastricht. They were nagged and coaxed
and bullied and chivvied along. The prime agency was the
Conservative Party, but less than a third of Conservatives who
voted for the Party in the 1987 election turned out for the
European elections in 1989.

A measure of the desperation felt by the continentalists over
tactics for the 1994 elections can be gauged from remarks to
constituency associations by Sir Christopher Prout, MEP:

> I would like to be able to say that we have been able, during the
> ensuing four years, to change the image of the European institu-
> tions in general and the European parliament in particular.
> However, I fear I cannot ... It will come as no surprise to you to
> learn that the views of a substantial number of committed
> Conservatives about the European parliament remain those that
> they held when they failed to turn out to vote at the time of the
> 1989 elections. Too many see the election of a Conservative
> candidate to the European parliament as capable of advancing
> neither their own nor their country's interest.[1]

In 1993 the European Conservatives affiliated themselves to
the pro-federalist European People's Party, hailing this as an
achievement in the battle against Euro-centralism. It did not
seem to strike them as odd, or worthy of discussion among
voters at home, that the programme of the EPP calls for a
federal Europe. 'A federal Europe is now more than ever a
necessary and realistic political objective ... It is realistic because history is speeding up [*sic*] and the people are ready for
the acceleration of a process of union based on delegation and
sharing national sovereignty.'

In this 'speeding up' of history Britain has fallen victim, not
to her separation from the world, but to an indiscriminate
embrace of its worst features, while at the same time any
distinctiveness she enjoyed from her island status has come
under the most intense assault. The British tolerated this
attack in the belief that they had no option other than to adapt.
The problem with this response is threefold. First, it prompts
the question how far the decline has to run and when, if ever, it

will end. Secondly, to the extent that the response has been one
of adjustment rather than remedy, the fact of decline is self-
willed and self-fulfilling. For want of vision and leadership,
Britain has wished it upon herself. And thirdly, it has made
Britain tolerant of an economic and social deterioration which
has nothing to do with her 'inheritance' at all but which lies
within her gift to rectify.

Britain and her people are being brought to a watershed. The
challenge is so serious and substantial that conventional policy
response will no longer suffice. She has already been forced by
huge tax increases to re-think not only the role of the state –
what it is that government should and should not do – but what
sort of nation she wishes to be – if an independent nation at all.
She is being forced to make an honest inventory of herself. But
even from this there is a drawing back for fear of the empty
cupboard that may be laid bare. Yet there is more here by way
of assets than liabilities – a fact to which relentless criticism
and decrying of Britain's past and her achievements has blinded
her.

Fundamental to any inventory is the possession of a unique
and unalterable treasury. Britain's greatest asset is the mind-
set of island. This has shaped her history, economy, institutions
and culture: gifts of destiny and inheritance that are beyond
price. It accounts, more than any other condition, for Britain's
independence, for the growth of her sovereign institutions and
for a culture that has taken the people's freedom to order their
affairs in a manner of their own choosing as an established and
inviolable right. This torch of freedom has burned bright in
Britain and inspired the world. While the fact of being an island
made the British in some respects an inward-looking, private
and diffident people, relatively unmoved by the ideologies and
political fashions that swept over Europe, it also brought forth
a global trading outlook.

Because of this outward impulse she came to preside over a
world empire. Indeed it destined her to be one of the world's
richest and most successful nations. Empire was the product
less of ideological mission – keenly felt though that was well into
this century – but of that strange alter ego of the insular British:
the unplanned, haphazard amalgam of Christian mission, liberal high-mindedness, gunboat diplomacy and joint stock ad-
venturism. It was how Britain came to sustain the Empire

'show' in the way that she did, and for the length of time that she did, rather than its size and power, that caught the world's imagination and made her 'great'.

These qualities of adaptiveness, resourcefulness, independence and respect for freedom and stability were formed out of the historical experience of being an island, rather than being imposed in the European way by written constitutions and Napoleonic codes laying down rules of conduct to be enforced by an elaborate government apparatus reaching into every corner of life. It is the absence of these that distinguishes Britain and 'Britishness'. Her people have had the most deep-seated beliefs, but they are among the most unideological people on earth. Their attachment to individual freedom and sovereignty grew not from a body of doctrine but out of a pragmatism tested by centuries of independence. No one taught the British the values of constitutional liberalism in some faculty of political science. It is how they are.

This defining characteristic of being an island, prompting a world outlook, has created and moulded her identity. It has moulded Britain's economy, and in particular the twin legacy of that invisible financial empire of overseas portfolio and direct investment that maintained its vibrancy long after her visible trade went into decline, together with skills in banking, insurance and financial services that have made London a preeminent financial centre.

But as much as by forces within as by those outside, Britain is being stripped of her defining consciousness. Since the 1960s the country's political leadership, initially encouraged by the United States, looked increasingly to Europe to secure her political and economic survival. Membership of the EC in 1973, followed by the signing of the Single European Act, were hailed as triumphs by a Whitehall Establishment devoid of indigenous solutions and increasingly acting out of an inferiority complex. At the same time the Foreign Office feared exclusion from a new Franco-German axis that seemed to be welding Europe into a regional super-bloc with global power pretensions.

To the Establishment and the professional middle class there was no sense of loss at the surrender of sovereignty. On the contrary. There was a vague perception of gain, that we could not do worse than we had done on our own. Economically, politically and culturally there seemed little to lose. Was there

any longer a national consciousness to be compromised by
European 'integration'? Had it not altogether lost its potency to
unify? Had not its expression, like that of the monarchy, become
ceremonial only? And was not economic performance so much
better in Europe – French planning, German technical prowess?

An infatuation with Europe and disdain for that which distinguished Britain from the continent characterised the elite
that took Britain into Europe. It seemed slow to notice that the
economies of Europe were deeply flawed; that the institutions
of the EC were small-minded and unaccountable; that the
Italian finances had all but collapsed; that the German economy, long past its post-war 'miracle', was in deep structural
crisis and prolonging recession across the continent; and that
on the drive back from its villas in the Provence the auto-routes
were lit up by the fiery road blocks and torched lorries of
truculent French farmers demonstrating against any GATT free-
trade agreement that would reduce their grants and subsidies.

Above all, in the abandonment of island consciousness no
thought was given to the unintended consequences of dismantling the ties of history; how in this vast new open pasture
without gates and fences and in which people could roam freely,
any social order could cohere. To what body of tradition and
values would people belong? Above all, what institutions and
values would interpose themselves between individuals and the
supra-national federal state? For once the national states were
stripped of their sovereignity and their *raison d'être*, there
would be no institution capable of standing up to the centre:
Britain would be in a terrain from which her parliamentary and
legal institutions had for so long protected her: a landscape quite
totalitarian. But down the slope she went, like so much cattle,
chicken-coops and debris floating down a river and out to sea.

The lure for Britain of increasing engagement in Europe was
at first less political than economic: the prospect of a single
market of 350 million people for goods and services, with free
movement across borders and attendant dramatic reductions in
distribution and transaction costs. We would enjoy the dynamic
benefits of this larger market. We would benefit from structural
funds. And later there came the ERM, that highway to the single
currency championed by the finest minds in those militantly
pro-EC Establishment bulletins, the *Economist* and the *Financial Times*. We would enjoy monetary and interest rate stability,

the preconditions for prosperity that had eluded successive British governments since the 1960s. What could go wrong?

Far from the EC presenting an expanding market for British goods, its share of OECD exports has declined over the past decade. It has become a high-cost, low productivity area increasingly vulnerable to competition from Asia and the Americas. There is nothing inevitable or assured about the future prosperity of Western Europe or its ability to attract global capital. None of Britain's economic problems is closer to being resolved. Indeed the more she has pursued convergence with Europe the more severe have the unaddressed domestic problems become. It is the breakdown of the Establishment pact with Europe – the 'done deal' under which Britain would cede sovereignty for economic benefit – that is now re-opening profound questions of Britain's purpose and place in the world.

It is the central argument of this book that Britain's salvation lies in rediscovering and building on her own past as a trading post for all the world, and not throw in its lot with a socialist and mercantilist regional bloc.

There is nothing about European convergence, either in the fast lane or in the slow, that offers any remedy to the predicament which Britain faces. Europe should not be used by Britain's political class for its own ambitions or to escape the truth that what is wrong with Britain can only be tackled by the British people, given confidence, vision and, above all, leadership. Nothing has more heightened the sense of 'inexorable' decline and ensured its realisation than Britain's abandonment of her past. That is at the root of her malaise. It is not just that she loses the wisdom of its lessons; it is that in losing her history she loses her future too.

Note

1. 'The choice in June 1994', by Sir Christopher Prout, MEP (Salop and Staffs) *Euro Brief*, June 1993.

2

Where We Are, Who We Are

We have no eternal allies and we have no perpetual enemies. Our interests are eternal and perpetual, and those interests it is our duty to follow.

Palmerston, 1848

In 1993, the year Britain signed the Treaty on European Union, the total of United Kingdom overseas portfolio investment in countries outside the European Community exceeded that for Europe and rose to an all-time record level. In that paradox can be found not only Britain's historical predeliction to be a global trader and investor but also evidence of the changed perception among City banks, investment institutions and private investors that the world's economic pulse was beating faster outside Europe.

The paradox points to an island country heading towards a new century with its identity and sense of place in the world under question as never before. Britain deeply desires the assurance of a stable and prosperous Europe. Her political, administrative and business elites do not want to lose out on influence at the heart of a continent that accounts for a large proportion of her overseas investment and trade. But she is a country deeply anxious after forty years of exhaustive debate on her place and role in the world. She senses that her economic and financial well-being ultimately flows, as it historically has always flowed, not from a continental regionalism, but from the freedom to invest and trade around the world; and what growth she currently enjoys stems less from convergence with the EC than from what the former Chancellor, Norman Lamont, chose to hail after the expulsion of Britain from the Exchange Rate Mechanism as 'a British policy for British interests'.

The matter of where we choose to do business and invest is central to the issue of our place in the world and 'who we are'. No issue is more critical: it is the very question of 'who we are' that has fired the continuing controversy over our relationship with Europe. The onset of Britain's crisis of identity can be traced to the debate in the early 1960s on whether to be, or not to be, a member of the European Community. By the unalterable fact of geography Britain has been both apart from Europe and also a major European power. From this ambiguity of 'who we are' has sprung a tension within the governing class between concern for British interests on the European continent and an outward global impulse, the prevalent dynamic since the first Elizabethan era.

Perceptions of where Britain's economic self-interest did *not* come to lie are as important in the definition of who we are as where they did. For example, though Britain is commonly referred to as a 'European power' and has played a decisive part in developments on the European continent, she has never regarded Europe as a theatre of empire or sought economic or political domination of its affairs.

Britain's economic self-interest was seen to lie in its development as an independent maritime power, trading with the continents of North and South America, Africa and the Middle and Far East. The history of Britain's continental involvement has never been one of imperial mission but rather one of thwarting the illiberal military imperialism of others and specifically of guarding against the continental Channel ports falling under the sole control of a potential aggressor. Free and unfettered access to the Channel has been the prime concern of British foreign policy since the reign of Elizabeth I. It remained so through the challenges of Philip II of Spain, Louis XIV and Napoleon into the early years of the twentieth century and the ascendencies of Bismarck and Kaiser Wilhelm.

It was this concern that dictated a complex and subtle diplomacy born of the requirement follow, in Palmerston's famous phrase, those 'eternal and perpetual interests'. Right up to the outbreak of the First World War it was a central concern of diplomacy that Britain should not find herself aligned with the dominant power in Europe. This reinforced a unique continuity of parliamentary sovereignty at home and the continuity of British commercial expansion overseas, strengthening both economic and political independence from the continent. It is no random whim of preference that British economic and commercial interests, while wishing to develop free trade with and within Europe, wish also to retain that flexibility and detachment, an unconscious echo of those precepts and traditions that have governed our outlook and thinking for generations.

From the seventeenth century Britain's economic and commercial interests found expression and fulfilment in almost every corner of the world. This expression was confined neither to trade in manufactured goods nor to the colonies of settlement but expanded into services and finance to an invisible empire embracing the Ottomans, southern Africa, the Far East and South America. This invisible empire of finance and services remained healthy and vibrant long after the pulse of trade in manufactured goods began to weaken. The period from 1870 is commonly regarded as one marked by the beginnings of decline in British trade and economic influence. Relative to Germany and the United States, the UK's visible balance of payments deteriorated sharply. From this point theories of our unalterable, 'systemic' decline began to take hold. The line is drawn of a relative, and then absolute, deterioration in our trade from around 1870 to the present day, explaining *inter alia* our inability to remain a sovereign economic power and the requirement to merge with a European economic and political bloc.

Yet this period was to mark the ascendancy of Britain's 'invisible' empire, with a huge expansion of finance, banking and trade in services. According to Cain and Hopkins in an outstanding study of Britain's financial empire,[1] between the periods 1851-75 and 1901-13 the UK current account in services rose from £59 million to £136 million and overseas investment income from £26 million to £151 million. After 1850 Britain became the centre for international finance, with profound repercussions not only for the pattern of overseas investment but for the character and composition of the British state.

British investment overseas was worth between £195 million and £230 million in the mid-1850s, rising to approximately £700 million in 1870, more than £2,000 million by 1900 and to between £3,500 million and £4,000 million by the outbreak of the First World War. This is not to suggest that there was a flight of confidence from domestic investment and manufacture: investors in this period preferred home to foreign investments and, as Cain and Hopkins noted, foreign stocks to imperial ones.[2] Manufacturers themselves were four times more likely to invest in a domestic company than a company overseas, and seven times more interested in domestic than imperial firms.

The investment appeal of empire is well understood. Less understood is the extent and power of Britain's invisible financial empire during this period. One of the most striking examples is South America, a theatre remarkably receptive to the combination of British economic power and liberal ideology. Britain's trade with Latin America grew threefold between 1865 and 1913. Latin America accounted for 10 per cent of Britain's exports between 1850 and 1913 and about the same proportion of imports. These proportions were larger than for any other continent or country within the empire, with the exception of India.

Even more striking was Latin America's role as the recipient of British capital. British holdings in the continent rose from a modest £81 million in 1865 to around £1,180 million by 1913. By that year Latin America accounted for 25 per cent of all British publicly issued overseas assets, a figure which put her in the front rank of international debtors in the non-industrialised world.

Even in China, arguably the last great underdeveloped market, British banking and finance had made substantial inroads in the early years of this century. Britain's share of inward direct investment rose from 66 per cent of the total in 1913 to 81 per cent in 1930 and grew further in the mid-1930s. In the early 1930s foreign banks headed by British firms, and by the Hong Kong and Shanghai Bank in particular, still financed over 90 per cent of the foreign trade in Shanghai. In 1936 Britain's investments in local manufacturing were also a long way ahead of those of any foreign country, including Japan.[3]

Some commentators have argued that this global impulse, of which empire was the most potent ideological expression, was some temporary aberration of the British people. 'For perhaps two decades', according to Paul Johnson, 'they allowed themselves to be enthused by the imperialist afflatus', which they came to discard 'with indifference, tinged occasionally with relief'.[4] But this is to pay scant regard to the importance and extent of Britain's financial and commercial empire. Equally, other analyses of this kind assume that this global impulse has long since played itself out and that British overseas economic interests have contracted to Europe. Recently it has become commonplace to assert that Britain is inextricably entwined with Europe: statements such as 'Europe accounts for the bulk of our trade' or 'Europe attracts most of our investment' or 'Our economic interests lie in Europe' pass as accepted coinage.

That the reality is different and altogether more complex is vital for us to understand, for the answer to the question of who we are is ultimately to be found in where we are and where we choose to trade and invest. British trade and investment around the world never recovered from the cost and trauma of two major European wars. But the size and range of her overseas assets are still substantial and far larger than the portfolios of other EC member states. The UK's total external assets currently stand at £1,300 billion (see table 2.3 on p. 26). Of this total, £467 billion consists of portfolio investment by institutions and private investors, and direct investments by companies are listed at £127 billion. Since these direct investments are listed by the Central Statistical Office at book value, a more accurate estimate of market value would put them at £250 billion* taking the total to just over £700 million – equivalent to the total current value of UK equity securities listed on the London stock market.

Where are these portfolio investments to be found? While a geographical analysis is available of Britain's visible trade, the CSO does not compile a geographical breakdown of invisible earnings, which is remarkable considering that receipts from invisibles exceed visible exports and are equivalent to more than 18 per cent of Gross Domestic Product, more than in any other major industrialised country.

However, figures are available for direct overseas investment (see table 2.1 on p. 24). Of the £127 billion total, £54 billion (43 per cent) is in North America; £25 billion (20 per cent) in the European Community (after stripping out the Netherlands where, as the CSO notes, figures are distorted by the operations of Dutch holding companies used by UK companies to invest in other countries); and £21 billion (17 per cent) in developing countries.

Australia, accounting for £8.5 billion or 9 per cent, dwarfs the total of the UK's direct investment in Germany (£4.9 billion or 3.8 per cent). Australia and South East Asia together at £15.5

*Research by Cambridge University Department of Applied Economics estimates market values for UK direct investment overseas at about twice book values. See *Overseas Investment, Capital Gains and the Balance of Payments* by Cliff Pratten, Institute of Economic Affairs Research Monograph 48, 1992.

billion account for more of our overseas direct investment than Italy, Greece, Denmark, Ireland, Luxembourg, Belgium, Portugal and Spain combined.

Analysis of our net earnings from direct investment overseas is also instructive (see table 2.2 on p. 25). To eliminate cyclical distortions, earnings for each of the five years 1987 to 1991 are aggregated to give a five-year total. An analysis of these figures shows that North America is again dominant, accounting for £25 billion or 35 per cent of the total for 1987-1991. South East Asia is the second largest with £7.5 billion (11 per cent), followed by the Caribbean and Latin America at £5.8 billion (8 per cent).

Together the Commonwealth accounts for £19 billion or 27 per cent of income from overseas direct investment; developing countries £17 billion (24 per cent) and the EC (excluding the Netherlands) £11 billion (16 per cent). Britain derives more direct investment income from Africa than she does from Ireland, Belgium, Luxembourg, Italy, Portugal, Denmark and Greece combined. Southern Africa now has the potential to be the economic power-house of the continent and in 1993 attracted substantial foreign equity portfolio investment. Lonrho, with interests spanning precious metals mining and agricultural products, represents the biggest British corporate presence in Africa and has an enormous UK investor following, with more than 200,000 shareholders.

The point is not that our EC direct investment and earnings are unimportant or declining – historically they have always been large and, it is to be hoped, will remain so – but that 80 per cent of overseas investment by asset and even more by earnings are derived from countries outside the EC and in economies that are now growing fast.

A similar picture emerges from an analysis of our net cross-border equity flows. Michael Howell, global equity strategist of Baring Securities, and Angela Cozzini set out how a Year 2000 private-investor portfolio was likely to look.[5] They forecast that almost half a typical British portfolio will be in developing countries compared with less than 8 per cent now.

But the haunting force of this Year 2000 portfolio is its familiarity for Britain. The model Barings used belonged to our grandfathers. It represented actual UK private-sector portfolio investments of 80 years ago. In 1913 about 53 per cent of British overseas equity investment was in 'emerging' stock markets.

We are now retracing these footsteps. Throughout 1993 there was a vigorous expansion of retail and institutional investment in emerging markets. Howell and Cozzini calculate that in 1993 total net overseas portfolio investment by UK investors in stock markets in Latin America, the Far East and other countries outside Europe, the US and Japan rose to a record £6.5 billion.

To avoid 'freak' one year totals, the figures for each of the years 1991 to 1993 are added together (see table 2.5 on p. 27). These give a revealing picture of today's UK investor preference. For investment in France the three-year total is £5 billion; for Germany £900 million; the corresponding figures for Latin America are £4 billion and for the Pacific Rim countries £6 billion. Thus, were a map of the world to be drawn showing the countries with the highest direct and recent portfolio investment nearest to our shores and countries with the least furthest away, North America would be where Europe is, Latin America where Africa is, South East Asia in the vicinity of Bermuda and Europe in the South Atlantic. It would also be a more revealing way to view the world after the December 1993 GATT agreement, with the strong-growth, low-cost areas of Asia and Latin America given prominence and the high-cost, high-regulation, low-growth countries of Europe de-emphasised.

Such a projection would also help dispel some myths about our trade with Europe. For example, it is said that 'more than half Britain's trade is with the EC'. But this is true only of her visible trade, which for each of the past ten years has accounted for less than half the total of our balance of payments, and even here the picture is changing with exports to non-EC countries catching up with those to the EC in the fourth quarter of 1993. The EC's share of our invisible trade credits is 35 per cent. Adding the totals of EC visible and invisible trade together gives a total of £9.8 billion or 45 per cent of our total current account. It would certainly give further cause to doubt the wisdom of linking the British currency to the Deutschemark, given that the bulk of Britain's overseas dealings is denominated not in marks but in dollars.

Britain's dependence on invisible earnings to make good the deficit on visible trade is by no means new. Between 1851 and 1913 Britain had a visible deficit but a much larger invisible earnings surplus. Moreover it is Britain's invisible trade surplus with the rest of the world that has helped to defray some, but not all, of the current account deficit with the EC, this totalling £87 billion since 1982 (a £72 billion deficit on EC visible trade and a £16 billion deficit on invisibles).

Of all Britain's assets, the most consistently under-rated has been the City of London (and, too often overlooked in general references to 'the City', the vibrant Scottish financial community in Edinburgh). In any inventory of the British national interest Britain's financial services and their colossal earning capacity would come close to the top of the list. Some 500 banks from 70 countries are located in London, compared with 280 in Paris and 250 in Frankfurt. Gross daily foreign exchange turnover in the UK averages $241 billion, more than a quarter of the global total. Some 19 per cent of international bank-lending is carried out through the UK, compared with 8 per cent in the United States and 7 per cent for both France and Germany. London has the largest stock exchange and foreign-exchange business compared with continental financial centres and is by far and away the biggest centre for Eurocurrency business.

Britain has built huge market shares in financial services activities (see table 2.7 on p. 28): in world-wide foreign exchange business it is estimated at 27 per cent; in world-wide mergers and acquisitions at between 40 and 50 per cent; in international equity under-writing at between 65 and 70 per cent; in Eurobond trading, 75 per cent and in institutional fund management 81 per cent.[6]

Growth in these areas in recent years has been explosive. Between 1986 and 1991, revenues from institutional fund management have leapt 135 per cent to £176 million; international mergers and acquisitions by 138 per cent to £368 million and foreign exchange business by almost three-fold to £1.8 billion.[7]

In equity trading London dominates Europe. A total of 1,878 companies are listed on the London Stock Exchange with a total market value of £700 billion. In addition, there are more than 500 listed overseas companies with a market value of more than £1,500 billion. Total London equity-market turnover rose from £405.2 billion in 1988, 6 per cent of the world total, to more than £760 billion in 1992 (10.4 per cent). London accounts for almost 60 per cent of all overseas equity trading. The equivalent share of New York is 27 per cent, of Switzerland 2.5 per cent and of

Germany 1.4 per cent. It also accounts for 90 per cent of all cross-border trading in Europe.

Overall, invisibles of £108 billion in 1992 accounted for some 23 per cent of the UK's national income (a higher percentage than for Japan, the United States, Germany and France; see table 2.8 on p. 29). Of this total, services contributed £32 billion. The surplus on private sector invisibles in 1992 came to more than £12 billion.

Nor, by asserting her skills in world trading and her determination to maintain London as a pre-eminent financial services centre does that make us 'bad' Europeans. To quote City investment banker Stanislas Yassukovich:

> In many ways the UK is the most 'European' of the member states of the EC. Ours is the European language most spoken in the rest of the world. Ours are the European commercial traditions most copied. Ours are the European industrial corporations with the largest market capitalisation. Ours is the European financial centre with the largest business and influence in the world.[8]

Britain's global interest and perspective, represented both by these activities and by London's historic pre-eminence as a financial centre, geographically linking the east with America in the 24-hour-a-day trading global market, are less the product of any super-power status present or past than of the role of broker or intermediary between governments, institutions, enterprises and investors brought together in a free and independent market responsive to their needs and which they could trust.

It is ironical that the forces that are shaping the new century play directly to the strengths of Britain's past. We sailed and we traded and we bartered and we financed. This inheritance of a world outlook was the gift of 'island'. British capital led the surge of investment in China and South America in the second half of the nineteenth century. In South Africa she was the pre-eminent financier of the gold, diamond and platinum mining industries, and British corporate finance was instrumental in creating the most sophisticated investment banking and financial centre in the African continent. In economic terms the cutting-edge of British presence abroad was less a roll-call of British manufacturers than the merchant banks of Hambros, Barings, Kleinwort, N.M. Rothschild and Schroder.

Now the wheel of British overseas investment is turning full circle. Maastricht did not mark a new stage of UK-EC cross-border corporate investment or financial services integration – of that there has been far less than expected. Corporate and institutional investors alike have been voting funds away from the EC. For trade does not follow the exhortations of bureaucrats at the European Commission but the lowest production costs and the highest rate of return. British companies continue to be huge investors in the world outside Europe. They have long been big investors in the United States. But trade and investment in South East Asia is now rising sharply. According to the Oxford University Forecasting Group, Britain's trade with China and the Pacific Rim economies will double well before the end of the century and will outstrip the United States as a market for British goods. The group forecasts that between 1992 and 1998 British exports to the Far East will grow from 7 per cent of the total to 14 per cent.[9] The view is echoed by Roger Bootle, chief economist of Midland Global Markets. He expects imports from the Asia Pacific region to account for 20 per cent of the British total by the end of the century, with exports claiming almost the same percentage.[10] In 1993 UK exports to the Asia Pacific region rose by almost 30 per cent to more than £7 billion and exports to China were more than double their 1992 level.

The boom in China and the Pacific Rim economies is bringing a profound change to the profile of top British companies in terms of geographic analysis of turnover. Many leading companies such as GEC, P&O, Courtaulds, Johnson Matthey, Trafalgar, and BOC Group expect the Far East to account for between 20 and 30 per cent of turnover by the end of the century.

Figures from telecommunications to power generation giant GEC show a 29 per cent increase in sales in South East Asia to more than £500 million. For the shipping and construction group P&O, expansion in China and South East Asia is less a new adventure than – literally – a return to old haunts. Visiting Shanghai for talks on a container terminal project, group executives found the pre-war P&O building still standing. In 1993 the group took a 25 per cent stake in south China's largest container terminal and now manages the terminal at Ahekou Port on the west coast of the Shenzen economic zone.

Precious metals refining and processing group Johnson Matthey, the world leader in auto catalysts, has made South East Asia the prime target for investment. Through a joint venture it is building a new auto catalyst plant in Malaysia, and intends to enter gold refining in China. It sees group turnover in this region doubling in three years. The conglomerate BTR has announced that its Australian offshoot BTR Nylex is building a £121-million glass manufacturing plant in China. Glass giant Pilkington is another UK company to have announced a China plant, joining BOC, Courtaulds, United Biscuits and ICI. Leading food and drinks companies such as Unilever, Allied-Lyons and Guinness are also increasing their China and South East Asia sales and distribution networks substantially.[11]

More than half Britain's top 100 quoted companies derive more than 30 per cent of profits from overseas, but only 14 of these companies have more than 30 per cent of earnings coming from Europe. British investment in the European Community has fallen from 29 per cent of total overseas investment in the 1980s to 20 per cent.

From the beginning of the debate on Britain's European membership it was evident that the question of whether Britain was or was not to be a member of the EC resolved itself into the greater question of whether Britain was to be, or not to be, a sovereign state. The question strikes at the heart of her current predicament. She has chosen, and continues by the pattern of direct and portfolio investment, to be supportive of, but separate from, the continent of Europe. Nations do not have to be satellites of super-powers to be 'great nations' any more than great companies have to be subsidiaries of multinationals to be great performers. Just as Sir Henry Tizard warned us more than forty years ago, the enemies of greatness are the very trappings that go with aggrandisement.

Britain's companies and financial institutions, by virtue of a cast of mind shaped over generations, and by the voluntary allocation of billions of pounds, assert that Britain has other areas, and more promising areas, to do business with and to invest in. It would be reckless to discount this, and it would be foolhardy, in any acknowledgment, to suggest that in an inventory of Britain's economic interests, it somehow counts for nothing.

Notes

1. *British Imperialism*, vol. I: *Innovation and Expansion 1688-1914*, by P.J. Cain and A.J. Hopkins, 1993, p. 170.

2. Ibid., pp. 182-3.

3. *British Imperialism*, vol. II: *Crisis and Deconstruction*, p. 237 et seq.

4. Paul Johnson, *The Offshore Islanders*, 1972, p. 392.

5. *Cross-border Equity Flows 1992*, by Michael Howell and Angela Cozzini, Baring Securities 1993.

6. *Revenue from the City's Financial Services*, Subject Report IV, London Business School, for the Corporation of London, p. 6.

7. Ibid., p. 9 .

8. Stanislas Yassukovich, *City Concern over Maastricht*, 1993.

9. Oxford Economic Forecasting Group, quoted by Robert Tyerman in the *Sunday Telegraph*, January 30 1994, City Section, p. 1.

10. Roger Bootle, chief economist, Midland Global markets, quoted by Robert Tyerman in the *Sunday Telegraph*, January 30 1994, City Section, p. 1.

11. Jamieson & Tyerman, 'Britain: Eastward Ho', *Sunday Telegraph*, January 30 1994, City Section, p. 7.

TABLE 2.1
UNITED KINGDOM OUTWARD DIRECT INVESTMENT
BOOK VALUE OF NET ASSETS BY AREA/COUNTRY (1991)

country/area	amount (£m)	% of total
1. United States	48,208	38.0
2. Caribbean/South America	11,254	9.0
3. Australia	8,526	6.7
4. France	7,177	5.6
5. South East Asia	7,035	5.5
6. Canada	5,998	4.7
7. Germany	4,899	3.8
8. Spain	3,792	3.0
9. Italy	2,399	2.0
10. Belgium/Luxembourg	2,406	2.0
11 South Africa	2,235	1.7
Commonwealth	29,331	23.0
EC (ex Netherlands)[*]	25,025	19.7
Developing countries	21,341	17.0
World total	126,927	

[*] Netherlands distorted by operations of Dutch holding companies used by UK parents to invest in other countries, and borrowing and lending through Dutch subsidiaries of UK companies.

Source: *CSO Bulletin Foreign Direct Investment 1991*, Issue 28/93, April 1993.

TABLE 2.2

NET EARNINGS FROM DIRECT INVESTMENT OVERSEAS
BY AREA AND COUNTRY 1987-91 INCLUSIVE (£m)

country/area	totals (£m)	% of total
1. United States	22,524	32.0
2. South East Asia	7,535	11.0
3. Carib/South America	5,877	8.0
4. Australia	4,812	7.0
5. France	2,862	4.0
6. Germany	2,819	4.0
7. Canada	2,378	3.0
8. South Africa	2,255	3.0
9. Rest of Africa	2,255	3.0
10. Ireland	1,223	2.0
11. Belgium/Luxembourg	1,107	1.6
12. Italy	915	1.0
13. Portugal	503	0.7
14 Denmark	376	0.5
15. Greece	87	0.1
Commonwealth	18,798	27.0
Developing countries	16,774	24.0
EC (ex Netherlands)	10,840	16.0
Total	69,529	

Source: *CSO Bulletin Foreign Direct Investment 1991*, Issue 28/93,
April 1993.

TABLE 2.3
BRITAIN'S EXTERNAL ASSETS 1982-92 (£bn)

year	direct investment by UK cos./residents	portfolio investments	total[*]
1982	52	40.9	416
1983	57.8	59.7	486
1984	75.1	84.3	624
1985	69.4	99.3	594
1986	80.7	140.3	721
1987	85.3	113.0	695
1988	104.3	145.8	776
1989	124.0	215.3	959
1990	119.9	181.6	904
1991	129.9	235.3	949
1992	162.7	304.2	1,192

[*] Includes lending to overseas residents, deposits and lending overseas by UK residents, government assets abroad, official reserves and other external assets of UK government.

Q1 1993	173.3	353.7	1,261.7
Q2 1993	175.8	371.7	1,301.8

Source: *CSO Pink Book* and balance of payments statistics.

TABLE 2.4
NET OUTWARD DIRECT INVESTMENT BY UK COMPANIES
AREA/COUNTRY ANALYSIS 1987-91 INCLUSIVE (£m)

country/area	1987-91 totals (£m)	% of total
1. United States	37,005	46.0
2. France	5,094	6.0
3. Australia	5,009	6.0
4. Carib/South America	4,499	5.6
5. Canada	3,812	4.0
North America	40,316	50
Commonwealth countries	14,551	18
Europe (ex Netherlands)	14,043	17
Developing countries	9,541	12
World total	80,701	

Source: *CSO Bulletin Overseas Direct Investment 1991*, Issue 28/93, April 1993.

TABLE 2.5
NET PURCHASES OF OVERSEAS EQUITIES BY UK
INVESTORS 1991-93E CUMULATIVE

country	total net purchases ($bn)
United States	(5.11)
Japan	19.37
France	8.00
Germany	1.39
Latin America	6.06
Pacific Rim	8.47

Source: Baring Securities.

TABLE 2.6

INTERNATIONALISATION OF LARGE COMPANIES

Foreign sales as a proportion of total sales for firms with a turnover of more than £1 billion, based on 1991 figures.

country of residence	foreign sale %	firms in sample
Britain	55.8	95
France	48.6	58
Germany	51.8	48
Italy	52.0	7

Source: European Policy Forum.

TABLE 2.7

MARKET SHARES IN INVISIBLES

Activity	turnover (£bn)	market share (%)
Foreign exchange	£44,559.0	27
International equity underwriting	£8.7	65-70
Eurobond trading	£1,634.0	75
Bank lending	£793.0	18
International fund management	£58.7	81
International mergers and acquisitions	£24.7	40-50
Shipbroking	£0.47[*]	50

[*] Net revenue

Source: City Research Project, London Business School.

TABLE 2.8
FINANCIAL SERVICES AS PERCENTAGE OF
NATIONAL INCOME

Country	%
Australia	20.0
Canada	18.0
France	19.0
Germany	13.0
Italy	23.0
Japan	16.0
Netherlands	17.0
United Kingdom	23.0
United States	21.0

Finance, insurance, real estate and other business services as a
percentage of Gross National Product.

Source: City Research Unit, London Business School.

TABLE 2.9
BRITAIN'S ROLE IN WORLD INVISIBLES

	% share of world invisible receipts	invisible receipts as % of GDP
USA	16.4	4.8
UK	10.1	18.2
Japan	9.3	5.3
Germany	7.7	8.0

Sources: IMF, Balance of Payments Yearbook.

3

Britain and a World in Change

The issue is not a mean one. It is whether you will be content to be a comfortable England, modelled and moulded on Continental principles and meeting in due course an inevitable fate, or whether your sons, when they rise, rise to paramount positions, and obtain not merely the esteem of their countrymen but command the respect of the world.

Benjamin Disraeli, Crystal Palace, June 24 1872

Three forces of unprecedented change are sweeping across the world in the 1990s, altering the landscape for a new century and a new age. They are unleashing the promise of a global boom without precedent with the potential to reshape the world.

The continuing shock-waves from the collapse of the former Soviet Union; the growing importance of the emerging market economies of Latin America and the Far East, China in particular; further trade liberalisation through GATT; and the explosion in cross-border flows of global finance: these changes, and the interplay between them, carry profound implications for all countries and for all regional economic blocs.

David Roche, global strategist at Morgan Stanley, sees the seismic change in terms of developed countries under challenge from adjacent hinterlands:

A decade ago there were one billion people in the free market system. Now there are five billion. Every rich economic bloc now has its hinterland of cheap skilled labour which dwarfs its own labour force in size and underwhelms it in cost competitiveness ... This represents one of the most dramatic transfers of pricing power, this time the pricing power of labour, that the world has ever seen.[1]

The economist Brian Reading has forecast that it is possible for real incomes to double by the year 2013 in countries accounting for 70 per cent of the world's population and 44 per cent of world output:

> Add in central Europe and the former Soviet Union and these numbers rise to three quarters and a half. If these numbers seem outrageous, it need only be noticed that six countries – China, India, the former Soviet Union, Indonesia, Brazil and Mexico – account for over half the world's population and a quarter of its GDP. Every one of them is likely to exceed 3.5 per cent a year real income growth over the next two decades.[2]

Yet at the heart of British policy has been the view that the world economy was polarising around three major geo-political blocs: the 'triad' of Europe, North America and Japan. This polarisation, aided by the increasing mobility of capital and the growth of multinational corporations, was seen as centralising, inevitable and accelerating. The developed world had increasingly come to be viewed through the eyes of the multinational corporation with its push for global marketing and cross-border division of labour.

In the 1970s and 80s the multinationals developed through this triad perception of the economic universe, seeking assembly plant or sales and marketing representation in one, both or all three of these blocs. As cross-border trade and investment grew, the triad stood to become increasingly dominant, increasingly interdependent and, within their respective jurisdictions, increasingly homogeneous. In this, the powerful conduit for change was cross-border finance and investment flows. During the 1980s foreign direct investment flows grew rapidly. By 1992, according to the United Nations World Investment Report,[3] the global stock of Foreign Direct Investment (FDI) had reached $2 trillion, generating $5.5 trillion in sales by overseas subsidiaries. By the early 1990s there were 37,000 multinational corporations with more than 170,000 foreign subsidiaries, some 90 per cent headquartered within the triad. The economic power of the multinationals is also highly concentrated. Roughly 1 per cent own half the FDI stock or total external subsidiary assets. The largest 100 corporations account for roughly $280 billion of the world stock of outward investment in 1990, or 14 per cent in total.

Britain in this period was increasingly drawn in to the process of European integration, less through any domestic

enthusiasm than the need to be competitive and fear of missing
out on the dynamic benefits and marketing opportunities that
these cross-border investment flows would bring to her multinational companies. Within the European bloc the process of
economic, monetary and political convergence and the reduction
and eventual elimination of employment, trading and currency
barriers have been encouraged to enhance Europe and to attract
vital foreign investment.

From this perspective two conclusions followed. The first was
that the process of European integration was irreversible and
that any slippages in the timetable for economic and monetary
union would, in the greater sweep of things, prove temporary.
The second was that Britain's economic interest lay in acceding
to this process of integration and harmonisation. It was this
sense of Britain being pulled into one of the powerful pillars of
the triad that gave the process a sense of historical inevitability
and unstoppable momentum.

What, therefore, do these three forces of change and the
interplay between them mean for Europe? Will they enhance or
detract from the process of economic convergence and centralisation? And what are their implications for Britain, already a
considerable way down the convergence route?

For Europe 1989 and the collapse of the Soviet Union marked
a turning point as momentous as those of 1815, 1917 and 1945.
In Eastern Europe a new order has struggled to emerge from
the unstable, fissiparous disintegration of the old. Russia itself
has undergone a political and economic implosion, currency
instability and deep division between it and its former satellites.
The switch from a centrally planned, military-command supra-
national economy to locally accountable, if highly unstable and
transient-looking, local administrations has brought traumatic
dislocation, inflation, widespread shortages and unemployment. It has also rewritten the map of Europe. This has altered
key assumptions about the future of the industrialised world
and Western Europe in particular. It has brought a crisis of
identity throughout Eastern Europe in the scramble to set up
new independent states.

But it has brought, too, a crisis of identity for Western
Europe. As the economies of the east applied to join the EC, the
club was faced with the most searching questions: What was to
be understood by the 'European Community?' How far was it to

extend? For if a 'community' cannot agree among itself what its boundaries are, where it begins and where it ends – those basic definitions without which there cannot be a 'community' – how deep could the process of economic and political integration within the EC now go?

The initial response to the liberation of the east – the reinforcement of barriers to the entry first of products and then of people – was that of a protectionist bloc fearful of the consequences for its economy and its political institutions. But the bloc itself did not have the assured political cohesiveness or will to act that its leaders supposed. The failure to develop a common foreign policy over the conflict in former Yugoslavia, looking instead to America for leadership, was one issue which posed questions over its federalist ambitions. The turbulence of the early 1990s was cited by many as all the more reason for Britain to look to Europe and to press on with convergence. But Europe has been slow to grasp the significance of this global shift of trade and capital allocation as the drama of the collapse of the Soviet Empire unfolded on its eastern border.

Central and Eastern Europe, freed from the grip of Comecon economics, quickly became a patchwork quilt of independent states, each with its own government, parliamentary assembly, diplomatic corps and representation at the United Nations. While their economies were severely handicapped by political uncertainties, technological underdevelopment and a culture which had suppressed entrepreneurial initiative, they also offered the potential of huge new markets for western goods and exceptionally low wage and production costs. An analysis by Morgan Stanley and McGraw-Hill[4] cites six Eastern European countries among the ten lowest labour-cost economies of the world.

Thus it was that the United States, committed to Western European union in the era of the Cold War, led an initial stampede of investment into Central and Eastern Europe: of the $2 billion of foreign direct investment in Poland between 1989 and 1993, $870 million or 44 per cent came from the US; $550 million of $1.9 billion foreign direct investment in the Czech Republic came from the US.[5] The initial investment rush simultaneously contributed to the growing doubts over the future composition and boundaries of the EC bloc.

The forces unleashed, far from centripetal, were centrifugal in both intent and effect. The wonder is not so much that it took the world so long to grasp their longer-term significance as that the Soviet Union, a federal super-state held together by the most extensive propaganda, police and security intelligence in the world collapsed as it did, and with the speed it did.

By 1985 the failure of the Soviet economy was manifest. Even in agriculture, where it had every natural endowment to enable self-sufficiency, the system's deficiencies required the importation of $20 billion of food a year. By 1990 only 150 out of a list of 1,200 basic consumer items were regularly available in shops.[6]

Yet initial hopes of a 'new world order' brought about by a speedy transition to a market economy were to give way to doubts in the West and concern that the eager support for fast transition and the ensuing dislocation may have put the reform process in jeopardy. A much more prolonged and painful transition looks inevitable.

The second seismic change has been the emergence of the Pacific Rim and China in particular as major economic players. A fundamental tilt in the balance of global economic power has gathered pace. Both by movement of capital through cross-border investment flows and by movement of assets and plant, the leadership of the world economy is shifting underfoot, away from the West and towards the East and South. The emerging economies of the Asian tigers, and to a lesser extent those of Latin America, have been gaining world market-share while Europe's has declined.

Evidence of this global shift of power and resource, with its pressing implications for Europe, has become a regular feature of International Monetary Fund and World Bank reports. Net flows of external capital to all developing countries in 1993 are forecast by the World Bank at $177 billion, against $157 billion in 1992, itself a record. China is the single largest recipient of foreign direct investment among developing countries. The total is estimated to have reached a record $27 billion in 1993. The bank has forecast that by the year 2002 the Chinese economic area will have experienced a fourfold explosion in gross domestic product. At standard international prices its GDP will have overtaken America's and will be three times the size of Germany's. According to a study by Baring Securities, by the year

2040 more than half the world's wealth will be produced around the Pacific Rim against a quarter today.[7] On Reading's projection, the years 1993 to 2013 could see China's share in world GDP more than double, from 7.5 per cent to 16 per cent, and Asia's rise from 20 per cent to 36 per cent. Meanwhile the OECD share could fall from 55 per cent to just 35 per cent.[8] These changes have been triggered by technology, demographics and politics. With the end of the Cold War, America no longer commands the obeisance in trade and finance as once it did from countries who relied on it for defence: they are freer to 'go their own way'.

At the same time the Japanese economy is experiencing, under the convulsions of a share, property and asset-price deflation, a complex 'scooping out' of plant and assembly to its Pacific Rim neighbours. World trade patterns are changing radically as a result, reshaping in particular the strategies of the multinationals. Trade within eastern Asia is growing faster than that within Europe and North America, while eastern Asia trade with the rest of the world is soaring and causing growing imbalances. Previously many countries in South East Asia produced low-priced and low-quality goods. With the help of capital inflows from the west these countries are now producing low-priced, high-quality goods, posing a serious competitive threat to Western companies, particularly in Europe, adding to deflationary pressures.

Thus the notion that the triad bloc will come to exercise an increasingly dominant magnetic pull of capital and plant now looks questionable. America has been suffering a spiralling trade deficit, forecast to reach $110 billion in 1994. More than half is with Japan. Its second largest is with China. Europe's trade deficit is also spiralling and its share of world trade diminishing. The scale of the Far East advance has been remarkable. Between 1980 and 1992 its share of world GDP has risen from 17 per cent to over 25 per cent, making it the world's most economically powerful region after the United States.

Within this total the pace of the advance of the 'tiger' economies excluding Japan has been breathtaking. Their economies over this period have grown by 182 per cent, outstripping the growth of any advanced industrial nation. The 'tiger' block as a whole now has a GDP larger than Canada's, and larger than those of Holland, Belgium, Sweden and Denmark combined.

This huge geo-political change will also see capital moving out of the OECD countries to finance growth in the investment-hungry emerging economies. In the years 1989-91, around one in every five new investment dollars was put into emerging Latin American and Asia Pacific stock markets. In 1993 this is estimated to have reached one in two.

Investment flows, which have risen sixfold in five years, are far outstripping the inflow of funds into the EC economies. Including venture capital and direct capital investment, the flow into Asian and Latin American markets came to more than $26 billion.

The West, and Europe in particular, has been slow to grasp the magnitude of the change. Many commentators in the early 1990s bemoaned what they described as 'a world recession', as if all economies, not just those of Europe, have been afflicted. In truth, there has been no 'world recession'. Global output kept rising between 1990 and 1993, and so too did world trade. In 1990 world trade grew by more than 5 per cent, in 1991 by 3.5 per cent and in 1992 by 4.7 per cent. Even across the Group of Seven nations, output continued to rise.

What has unfolded is a maturing of the miracle economies of the post-war generation – Germany and Japan in particular – and an increasing switch by investors to those economies engaged in a quantum-leap catch-up with the triad. Thus, not only the magnetic pull of the global triad but its claims to hegemonic status are coming under challenge from forces which look as 'historic' and 'inevitable' as those claimed for the triad bloc. As for cross-border financial flows acting as an accelerator for convergence within the triad, the dynamics would appear to be double-edged. The growing facility for cross-border finance which has created, *inter alia*, huge speculative flows in and out of currencies to the destruction of fixed or semi-fixed rate regimes, arbitrates between, rather than supports, the centralising drive of the triad blocs.

In the advanced Western countries policy co-ordination has all but broken down. Despite years of summitry by the Group of Seven nations to achieve co-ordination, the chief characteristic of the world economy is its divergence and the disparity of economic experience. Indeed it is de-synchronisation, not co-ordination, that offers the best prospect for recovery.

It is not only the flow of funds to the emerging markets but also the rates of economic growth that have significance for Europe. In Latin America (excluding Brazil) Gross Domestic Product grew by a meagre 1.8 per cent in the 1980s. In 1992 growth jumped to 4.3 per cent and was on target to rise a further 3 per cent in 1993. Chile, helped by structural reforms and privatisation, enjoyed growth of almost 10 per cent in 1992 and was on course for 7 per cent in 1993.

The resumption of growth in Latin America is not the result of 'piggybacking' on a boom in the industrialised nations, or a raw materials or commodities price boom, but of stabilisation and reform programmes that have reduced inflation, improved efficiency and increased supply. William Brown, chief economist at J.P. Morgan, reported:

> By 1991 every major country in the region except Brazil had taken steps to replace inward-looking, statist policies with programmes to open their industries to competition and reduce the role of government in their economies. In a vote of confidence in the reforms, large-scale capital inflows to the region resumed.[9]

The reasons for the boom in the Pacific Rim are altogether more complex than in Latin America. Far from there being a sudden 'Big Bang' of growth, the momentum has been building for some time. In the 1980s Hong Kong, South Korea, Malaysia, Singapore, Taiwan and Thailand all achieved growth rates of between 6 and 9 per cent. China's rate of growth exceeded 8 per cent. By comparison, the EC grew at 2.2 per cent.

In 1992 China achieved a near-13-per-cent growth surge accompanied by a jump of more than one third in fixed investment and a rise in industrial production of more than a quarter. Exports rose by over 18 per cent. While a slowdown is inevitable, there is a sense that China has embarked on a momentous change in its economic power and its standing in the world. Roche concluded after a visit in 1993 that 'investing in China's future will be the world's most profitable investment opportunity for the next ten years'.[10]

The growing share of world trade enjoyed by the Pacific Rim economies is especially marked in high-technology exports where the combined shares of Japan, Hong Kong, South Korea, Singapore and Taiwan rose from 8 per cent in 1970-73 to 25 per cent in 1988-89. Over this period the United States' share fell

from 30 per cent to 20 per cent and the combined shares of
Germany, Britain, France and Italy from 38 to 30 per cent.

Dr Walter Eltis, chief economic adviser to the President of
the Board of Trade, has identified three causes: an ability to
develop reliable high-technology products and to manufacture
on a large scale at competitive prices; high savings-ratios,
mostly over 30 per cent of GDP; and (with the exception of
China) low public expenditure, an absence of budget deficits and
a similar absence of European taxes on employment.[11]

The Western industrialised countries, particularly the
United States, have recognised the potency of these developing
economies through the phenomenon of 'out-sourcing' – the
transfer of manufacturing plant to countries where employment
and production costs are sharply lower. Wall Street economist
Henry Kaufman argues that this is the greatest challenge facing
the advanced industrialised nations:

> Looking at the liberated economies of Eastern Europe out-
> sourcing will be a very important economic test for the survival
> of basic industries in Western Europe. It is my belief that this
> re-structuring will be felt through the whole of the industrialised
> world.[12]

For Britain, increasingly drawn into European integration in
the belief that three-way global regionalism has an unstoppable
momentum, the rise of the emerging market economies and the
surge in global investment flows to the east and south are
undermining the assumptions that have guided policy. Not only
are the arguments that made us turn to a European regional
destiny losing their potency but the economic imperative behind
them is being overtaken. The aggregate effect of the changes
now unfolding appear to be less centralising but centrifugal. The
collapse of the Soviet system is a dramatic example of the
centrifugal deconstruction of one of the world's largest supra-
national economic and administrative empires. At the same
time the rise of the emerging market economies challenges
rather than strengthens the economic pulling power of the triad
bloc, as it also raises the question whether the British economic
interest is best served by throwing in the towel with an uncompetitive and cost-burdened producer bloc. Yet, despite these
growing doubts, the prevailing argument is that Britain would

find it impossible to survive on the periphery of Europe, let alone outside it, and that the process of harmonisation and integration should continue.

This argument takes a forgetful, if not a cavalier, view of Britain's position and her history. It pays scant regard to the fact that for several decades Britain has received more American and Japanese foreign direct investment than any other member of the EC, both countries having placed 40 per cent of their respective overseas investment in the UK.[13] The reasons most frequently given are language, absence of foreign exchange controls, the lowest rate of corporation tax in the EC and labour costs substantially lower than in France, Germany, the Netherlands, Italy and Spain. In truth, it is not because of our convergence with the EC but because of our continuing differences that investment has come to Britain.

Britain's greatest asset, in hard currency as much as predisposition and spirit, has been its global outlook. This world view, which first took shape with the development of trade in the sixteenth and seventeenth centuries, has echoed down the years. Prominent in any definition of Britain's national interest is the pre-eminence of London as a global financial and trading centre. To the question 'What is it that Britain can do, or what service can it provide, that is different from, or better than, those of its competitors?', the answer at the top of the list would be its skills in financial services – currency dealing, cross-border bond and equity trading, portfolio management, trade finance and insurance: in short, those 'invisible' activities which generate annual revenues of around £20 billion. London has already benefited hugely from the quantum leap in cross-border equity flows.

By contrast continental Europe sees itself not as an intermediary in this sense but as a partisan – as one of the top three regional economic blocs. It thus views global trends and events from the perspective of whether they advance or set back the interests of that bloc. To those interests Britain is not unsympathetic. But with more than half its total overseas trade and services with countries outside the EC, and its corporate sector still by far the largest investor in the United States, Britain still stands – as broker and portfolio manager it historically could only stand – economically, culturally and politically apart.

In the five years to 1992 British exports to the Pacific Rim economies, while small in relation to our total, grew faster than our exports to the EC, America and the oil-producing economies. In 1993 Britain's visible trade with the EC showed a marked deterioration, with exports to the EC in the final quarter falling by 9.5 per cent while exports to the rest of the world rose by 3 per cent. For the year as a whole British exports to Japan and Australasia rose by 22 per cent, to the rest of the world (including the Pacific Rim and Latin America) by 29 per cent, but to the EC by only 5 per cent.

The forces that are reshaping the world thus have profound implications for Britain. First, they provide an opportunity to draw on her history and her pre-eminence as a financial centre to be a major player in the growth of global financial services and trade finance. Secondly, they highlight the extent to which Britain's economic interests may be best served less by harmonisation and elimination of differences with continental Europe than by capitalising on these differences, particularly those which draw overseas direct investment. And thirdly, they put a question mark on the wisdom of Britain proceeding towards integration with an uncompetitive pillar of the triad which is losing world market share.

In aggregate these changes are unstitching the rationale of EC convergence for Britain as they have unstitched the rationale of a foreign policy dominated for a generation by the requirements of Western security predicated on political and military containment of the Soviet bloc. In an epochal change for the world economy, Britain requires more than ever a global vision.

Notes

1. David Roche, *The Challenge of Global Restructuring*, Morgan Stanley International Investment Research, September 1993, p. 1.

2. Brian Reading, *The Great World Boom 1993-2013*, *Britain & Overseas*, Autumn 1993; see also *Lombard Street Research Monthly International Review*, August 1993, p. 3.

3. *World Investment Report 1993: Transnational Corporations and Integrated International Production*, United Nations, New York, 1993, p. 1.

4. Morgan Stanley, *Global Strategy and Economics*, 1993.

5. Information kindly supplied directly by Morgan Stanley.

6. See an instructive analysis by William Keegan, *The Spectre of Capitalism*, 1992, chs 4 and 5.

7. Michael Howell, *Cross-Border Capital Flows: A Study of Foreign Equity Investment*, Baring Securities, 1993.

8. Reading, op. cit., p. 9.

9. William Brown, *Emerging Markets Quarterly*, Spring 1993, J.P. Morgan.

10. See David Roche, *China! Report on the Morgan Stanley Tour of China* for an outstanding analysis of investment prospects, p. 1: Executive Summary.

11. Walter Eltis, *Bank Credit Analyst*, 1992.

12. Henry Kaufman in an interview with the author, New York, October 1992.

13. *UK Technological Competitiveness: The Influence of Inward and Outward Investment*. Parliamentary Office of Science and Technology, July 1993.

TABLE 3.1

GROWTH AND SAVINGS: ASIA AND EC 1980-89

country	growth of GDP(%)	export growth (%)	savings as % of GDP
Japan	4.1	6.2	32
Hong Kong	6.6	14.1	30
Korea	8.7	11.0	31
Malaysia	5.8	9.7	34
Singapore	6.9	9.5	41
Taiwan	7.5	11.4	33
Thailand	7.2	12.9	23
China	8.5	11.8	35
EC	2.2	4.1	20
UK	2.1	3.8	17

Source: OECD and Bank Credit Analyst Publications.

4

The Collapse into Europe

I do not believe that this House would ever agree to our entering arrangements which, as a matter of principle would prevent our treating the great range of imports from the Commonwealth at least as favourably as those from other European countries. So this objection, even if there were no other, would be quite fatal to any proposal that the UK should seek to take part in a European common market by joining a customs union.

Harold Macmillan, 1956

I agree with the Chancellor that it is impossible for us to contemplate going into a full customs union. To do so would mean not only whittling down imperial preferences but introducing anti-imperial preference. That is a position manifestly impossible for any British government.

Roy Jenkins, 1956

The people must be led slowly and unconsciously into the abandonment of their traditional economic defences ...

Design for Europe, 1947

How did Britain come to perceive integration with Europe as the only means of political and economic survival? What was the process by which our destiny was seen to lie within what is now formally called the European Union? How did that perception come to be the dominant view of all the main political parties, the Treasury, the Foreign Office and the diplomatic elites? And what external influences contributed to this process?

The story of how Britain came to accept a European destiny is one less of enthusiastic embrace than of collapse – and one not all of Britain's making. How she came to be in the European Union is not an account of a national enthusiasm but of a grudging reluctance, a progression of doubts never fully overcome. The full implication of European union was for thirty years deliberately side-stepped or played down for fear of public outcry over the implications for national sovereignty. But even this does not do full justice to the complex interaction of external influences on a nation at a time when the confidence of its governing elite was at its most vulnerable. It is a story not of purpose or resolve, but of the breakdown of a compromised and enfeebled political Establishment.

What was the catalyst of that breakdown and who or what stood most to gain from what now seems, in retrospect, a very British coup? It was a process which in its early days was as clandestine in intent as it was furtive in procedure, a process that, in its inception, could truly only take place 'while Britain slept'. Indeed from the outset it was a requirement of those who envisaged a European destiny for Britain that the people should be led, according to one phrase, 'slowly and unconsciously' to that end, in the recognition that the full implications would never be acceptable.

The words were those of Lord Thorneycroft, a former Cabinet minister and chairman of the Conservative Party, in a booklet entitled *Design for Europe*, published in June 1947. The paragraph addressed 'the obstacles to European union':

> No government dependent upon a democratic vote could possibly agree in advance to the sacrifice which any adequate plan must involve. The people must be led slowly and unconsciously into the abandonment of their traditional economic defences, not asked, in advance of having received any of the benefits which will accrue to them from the plan, to make changes of which they may not at first recognise the advantage to themselves as well as to the rest of the world.

'Slowly and unconsciously' was to prove all too prophetic a description of how the subordination of Britain to a European supra-nationalism slipped into the mainstream of Conservative and Labour thinking. It also provided a premonition of the elitism that was to be a hallmark of the advocates of a federal Europe.

In presenting the history of Britain's approach to Europe as other than what it was, the British continentalists conveniently allowed a series of legitimising myths to settle in the public mind. The first was the myth of historical inevitability of the process of British integration with Europe and the presentation of Britain's relationship with Europe in the post-war period as one of natural and evolving convergence. The second was the myth that membership was in the national interest, as defined by economic benefit and national security objectives. And the third was the notion of a popular consensus in favour of convergence and integration with Europe, at least in principle. The corollary of this third myth was that opposition to the EC has always been marginal to the British political system and has never looked a credible option against a natural and voluntary preponderance in favour of membership.

It was to take almost twenty years, with the push for economic and political union represented by the Maastricht Treaty, for the full agenda of European integration to strike home. To the extent that this agenda was already known may be seen as a triumph of collective realism over the repeated assurances of top government ministers, both Labour and Conservative, who over the years denied that any substantial threat was posed to British nationhood and sovereignty.

Immediately after the Second World War the interests and destinies of Britain and continental Europe were amicable but divergent. The main impulse on the continent was to secure reconciliation between France and Germany; the broader goal was always European union. Britain, on the other hand, with an Empire and Commonwealth of 475 million people covering 20 per cent of the surface of the earth, had from the beginning a more global view. She had emerged from the war in a greatly weakened and indebted state but still as a leading industrial and political force, considerably stronger than any market economy other than the United States. The broad strands of policy could be traced to the official Foreign Office response to the Briand Plan for the union of Europe in 1930 which still 'lay on file' with no compelling reason to be changed:

> We warmly desire to improve the co-operation between European countries for the promotion of their common interests and will help to bring it about. We cannot, however, help to create any political or economic group which could in any way be regarded as hostile to the American or any other continent, or which would weaken our political co-operation with the other members of the British Commonwealth.[1]

While the emerging ideas on the continent were local, in the sense that they focused on European domestic requirements, for Britain three foreign policy requirements were paramount.

First was the defence and maintenance of her Empire and Commonwealth system of trade-preference to ensure the supply of raw materials for the rebuilding of her economy. Second was the maintenance of the 'special relationship' with the United States, both for purposes of defence and for global free trade. It was a complex alliance born of a need to mitigate tensions of interest between the two countries. Britain was still a global power with an Empire and Commonwealth bound by a trade-preference system that stood in the way of American expansionism. At the same time America had extended to Britain substantial loans during the war and, between 1948 and 1950, some $2.7 billion in Marshall Aid, equivalent in 1994 value to £12 billion. America saw the alliance as a foreign-policy means to secure influence in Europe. Britain saw it as a means of defusing, or at least containing, America's long-standing determination to dismantle the system of Commonwealth preference. This tension between the United States and Britain was to assume critical importance.

The third requirement was the encouragement of a reconciliation within Europe. There was a goodwill towards the knitting together of Europe and a wish to support reconciliation, but never a desire to become subservient to a supra-national European vision. Thus was formed what became known as the three interlinking circles of British post-war policy: the Commonwealth, Europe and the Atlantic Alliance.

Churchill frequently proclaimed the need for European unity and British goodwill for that aim, but always stopped short of British integration into a European union. The key to the attitude of successive British governments lay in a subtle but vital understanding of prepositions:

> But we have our own dream and our own task. We are with Europe but not of it. We are linked but not combined. We are interested and associated, but not absorbed.[2]

What did this mean in effect? Two eloquent summations have been left of the broad thrust of British foreign policy shared by both parties in the immediate aftermath of the war. The first came from the redoubtable Ernest Bevin, Foreign Secretary in

the post-war Attlee government, who emphasised the importance of the Atlantic Alliance. Membership of a European supra-
national body leading to federal institutions formed no part of
British aspirations:

> Europe is not enough; it is not big enough, it is not strong enough
> and it is not able to stand by itself. It is this great conception of
> an Atlantic Community that we want to build up.[3]

The second was that of Lord Avon (Anthony Eden) in his
memoirs *Full Circle*:

> We continuously encouraged close co-operation and unity be-
> tween the continental powers but we did so from the reserve
> position that the world would not accept a sovereign European
> authority ... others found this outlook patronising and irritating
> ... but we have a different and distinct outlook. This is because
> as a people we prefer to see how a principle works before we
> enshrine it, if we ever do so.[4]

But on the continent ambitions centred on economic and
political integration, with a federal supra-national authority as
an ultimate goal. The first organised body set up to campaign
for a united states of Europe after the war was the European
Union of Federalists, established in December 1946. Its first
congress in The Hague in 1948 led to the formation of the
Council of Europe, which in turn gave birth to the European
Commission on Human Rights and the European Court of
Human Rights.

The next landmark was the European Coal and Steel Community, founded by Jean Monnet, a French civil servant. He
believed that co-ordinated planning could be applied on a European scale, starting with one or two sectors. If governments
could be persuaded to surrender sovereignty over these, they
could be persuaded to surrender control over others and thus,
in the words of historian Stephen George, 'create, without ever
making a decision to do so, a European economy by piecemeal
surrender of control, sector by sector'.[5] The first two were to be
coal, which was in short supply, and steel, which was in surplus.
The plan was endorsed by Robert Schuman, the French foreign
minister.

French insistence that all participants should commit themselves in advance to the principle of supra-nationalism guaranteed British rejection – the first of three major and unambiguous decisions by Britain. Thus Harold Macmillan, the most pro-European politician of the period:

> One thing is certain and we may as well face it. Our people will not hand over to any supra-national authority the right to close down our pits and our steelworks.[6]

Britain's second rejection of European integration came in the critical area of defence. This time the mainspring of the proposal was, most tellingly, American. Faced with war in Korea and an increasingly onerous military involvement in South-East Asia, the United States sought to encourage the rearmament of Germany and linked the commitment of further American troops in Europe to the achievement of that aim. The outcome was the Pleven Plan of 1950. This proposed the creation of a European army, a European defence budget and a European defence minister answerable to a European assembly. Churchill was opposed and Eden had no wish for Britain to become a member. 'The implication,' as George noted, 'that if Britain joined, it would have to merge its armed forces into a European army was too alarming a surrender of national sovereignty – even [he added archly] for the Foreign Office to contemplate.'[7]

The controversy prompted Eden to remind the world that Britain, while not opposed to European co-operation and Europe-wide defence initiatives, did not wish to see its foreign policy and its armed forces become part of a European apparatus. 'What you've got to remember,' a close official recalled Eden saying, 'is that if you looked at the postbag of any British village and examined the letters coming in from abroad to the whole population, ninety per cent of them came from beyond Europe.' We were brought back by Eden to the prepositions:

> We are not members of the European Defence Community, nor do we intend to be merged in a federal European system. We find we may have a special relation to both. This can be expressed by prepositions, by the preposition 'with' but not 'of' – we are with them, but not of them.[8]

Britain's third major distancing from closer European ties now came over the decision not to join a European customs union. This reflected the importance of the Commonwealth preference system to Britain: around 80 per cent of Britain's trade on the eve of the war had been carried out with the preference-area countries, and these accounted for considerably more than half her exports. Even by the mid-1950s it formed the hub of the world's largest trading organisation outside the Soviet empire, accounting for 25 per cent of world exports and 30 per cent of imports.

The strongest challenge to the system of Commonwealth preference had come from the United States. From the 1940s the American State Department had been bent on its dismantling, together with the abolition of the role of sterling as a reserve currency, in order to remove barriers to the penetration of American equipment and products. The campaign reached its climax in the immediate post-war period when Britain was most in need of the system that had helped her recover from the 1930s slump.

The idea of Britain joining a European customs union was never seriously accepted as a policy option. The then Chancellor, Harold Macmillan, warned that the Commons would never agree to enter into arrangements under which European imports were treated more favourably than those of the Commonwealth. In 1956 he declared that Commonwealth trade 'would be quite fatal to any proposal that the UK should seek to take part in a European common market'. The view was endorsed by a young and promising Labour politician, Roy Jenkins, who said that to contemplate joining such a union would be 'a position manifestly impossible for any British government'. Thus in three main areas Britain had chosen to remain amicable to but apart from the continent, a course dictated by her commitments to the Commonwealth, the requirements of her world role and an intuitive preference for independence and non-interference in domestic affairs that reached back deep in the island consciousness to the Reformation.

The preferred link with Europe was not the political confederation conceived at Messina in 1955 by Monnet and Schuman but the European Free Trade Area which sought open trade but with no political superstructure. Few questioned that it was appropriate to stand apart from European political involvement, any more than they questioned that it was appropriate for Britain to have a world outlook and to think and act as a trading-post for all the world, not just one regional geo-political bloc.

The seismic event that was to shake these assumptions was Suez: not just the humiliation of Suez, but the behaviour of the United States. The political vacuum the debacle left in its train triggered deep heart-searching about Britain's post-war role and national identity. It was less a turning-point than a collapse – one MP at the time likened it to a collective nervous breakdown. It has had the most profound effect on thinking and attitudes for a generation.

In July 1956, two years after Britain had wound down her military base in Egypt, Colonel Nasser announced a decree nationalising the Suez Canal company. Britain was the biggest user of the canal: 25 per cent of all British exports and imports went through it, including half of all Europe's oil. Eden was on strong ground in resorting to the use of force, as Egypt was in breach of international law. But he bargained without opposition from the United States, where a Presidential election campaign was under way, with the Republicans committed to a peace platform. After considerable indecision, a plan was prepared by which French and British troops, following a pre-arranged attack on Egypt by Israeli forces, would repossess the canal under the pretext of separating the combatants.

On November 5, British and French planes bombed Egyptian positions. More than a thousand British and French paratroops were dropped outside Port Said and larger numbers invaded from the sea. The action provoked an outcry. At home Labour's Aneurin Bevan likened the attack to that of Germany on Norway in 1940, while Labour's deputy leader James Griffiths thundered: 'This is for our country a black and tragic week ... an unjustified and wicked war.' Most of the press opposed the operation. Eleven Conservative MPs rebelled and two ministers resigned. There was hostile international reaction. India's premier Nehru, normally a good friend of Britain, declared: 'I cannot think of a grosser case of naked aggression.' But the most telling opposition came from the United States.

President Eisenhower said the US 'was not consulted in any

phase of these actions which can scarcely be reconciled with the principle and purposes of the United Nations'. More sinister for Britain, as Lord Privy Seal Rab Butler later recalled, was a speculative run against sterling 'mainly in the American market or on the American account'. The Chancellor, Harold Macmillan, according to Butler, 'switched almost overnight from being the foremost protagonist of intervention to being the leading influence for disengagement – as well he might, for the loss of $279 million in that November represented about 15 per cent of our total gold and dollar reserves'.[9] To make matters worse, the US Treasury was opposing the request of Britain to withdraw capital from the International Monetary Fund, in which the US had a decisive say, to support the pound. Later the Americans agreed to an IMF loan to Britain if it agreed a cease-fire.[10]

Thus, with no option but to back down, Britain agreed to a cease-fire. The last British forces left Suez at the end of December. Eden, broken by the affair, resigned the premiership in January the following year. (This remains the prevalent account, though one biographer of Eden has suggested that the Americans demanded the Prime Minister's resignation and Macmillan, Butler and Churchill helped to engineer it.[11])

So ended what some regarded as the last Imperialist dance and others as 'a quest for civilised behaviour in a world of dissolving standards'.[12] Eloquent words have poured forth on how Suez exposed the collapse of British military and economic power and marked the end of her world role. But was it impotence of means, or irresolute will? Britain's representative at the United Nations, Sir Pierson Dixon, recalled:

> ... at the time I remember feeling very strongly that we had by our action reduced ourselves from a first class to a third class power. We revealed our weakness by stopping; and we threw away the moral position on which our world status largely depended. We were greater than our actual strength so long as people knew that we went to war in defence of principle ...[13]

The seizure of the canal struck directly at those codes of law and reasonable behaviour of which Britain had come to be seen as principal defender: 'the free movement of capital and goods,' as Professor Skidelsky summarised it, 'prompt payment of debts, the sanctity of contract, freedom of navigation, international peace and stability'.[14] These were the 'national interests' which Britain was to uphold 38 years later over the Falklands though with more resolute leadership than was displayed at Suez, and with a considerably more successful result.

Eden, who was born in 1897 at the height of Empire and who died in 1977 in an island then in hock to the IMF, came to personify a country and an elite in decline. Reading the accounts of the period between 1936 and 1956 when he was a force in British politics – the patina of 1930s charm and elegance crumbling by the end to reveal an ill, weak, irascible and often irresolute Prime Minister who buried himself in minutiae – it is hard not to see in Eden's full circle the oppressive atmosphere of Dartington Hall in Kazuo Ishiguro's haunting novel, *The Remains of the Day*: a once-grand mansion sliding into terminal decay but with the daily routine obliviously maintained. Of any sense of a need for renewal – of a need to re-order British purpose around the maintenance of sovereignty – there seemed little sign. For that patrician mediocrity and delusion, Suez was the final crash of masonry, the gaping hole as the roof fell in.

Suez also brought home the extent to which the United States was able to inflict a wound that shattered Britain's confidence in herself, not just as the protector of a global commonwealth but as a sovereign power. The consequences were both immediate and far-reaching. The first was a collapse of belief in Britain's ability to pursue an independent world role. The second, with the departure of Eden, was that British foreign policy came increasingly to be influenced by the US State Department and a Foreign Office anxious to find a new role. And the third was susceptibility to growing American pressure on Britain to join the Common Market.

From 1956 the Conservative Party was to turn to Europe both as a substitute for Britain's global consciousness and, increasingly, as a means of revitalising an economy exhausted by irreconcilable objectives: full employment, price stability and the funding of a huge and ever-expanding welfare system. For Britain, traumatised by Suez, there was no period of recuperative retreat during which it could assess the lessons and rationally scan the options available. That necessary re-appraisal was never undertaken. Instead, Europe came to fill the vacuum. That Britain, shorn of its east-of-Suez commitments, could survive and prosper with reduced political ambitions as an independent country cutting its coat to its cloth was never examined, both because of an unwillingness to come to terms with the scaling down of stature involved and because the United States was soon to come forward with its own pressing agenda.

In the chasm of Suez and its aftermath it suited the United States to consolidate control of Britain's nuclear deterrent and to advance her integration with Europe, thus enabling the US to counter Gaullist neutralism by proxy. According to the historian Richard Neustadt, the US not only wanted Britain to go in, but wanted Britain 'to go in there and dominate it on behalf of joint British American concerns'. After Suez, Britain was effectively a push-over for this agenda.

For the Conservative Party the switch on Europe was to require the surrender of its traditional appeal as the party of nationhood and patriotism and the adoption of a foreign policy centred on Europe. According to Douglas Evans in *While Britain Slept,*

> If such a complete reversal of traditional Conservative policy, not to say attitudes, were to be successfully achieved it would take a very long time – unless the conversion campaign was concentrated not on the party as a whole but on the decision-takers and the opinion-formers. In fact, that is precisely how it seems to have been conducted. But even a selectively concentrated campaign of this kind would probably have proved fruitless except for one major essential precondition – namely that the British political Establishment in the Conservative Party had broadly lost confidence in Britain's ability to solve her national problems. This particular consciousness can be dated fairly precisely to 1956-57.[15]

The 'cause' of the Common Market was never to be a popular, galvanising force in Britain, a rallying cry of its people or the occasion for spontaneous enthusiasm. Indeed the public was sceptical, and opinion polls in 1960 saw only a minority in favour of joining. Rather, it was the exclusive enthusiasm of a few in the Cabinet, the Foreign Office, the Washington Embassy and the Treasury: the top echelons most traumatised by Suez, where confidence in Britain was at its nadir. What Macmillan was counting on in 1960 to accomplish a silent revolution in the Conservative Party was less popular endorsement than acquiescence. Ministers hoped that somehow the Common Market would relieve them of their more intractable problems and galvanise Britain's sagging economic performance.

The central players in the Cabinet were Christopher Soames and Duncan Sandys, pro-marketeers whom Macmillan promoted. The critical figures in the diplomatic circuit were Lord Harlech and Sir Eric Roll. Both had served in the British Embassy in Washington and had become converts to Kennedy's vision of a Western European alliance in which Britain would be the leader of an enlarged EC.

At the Foreign Office Sir Con O'Neill drove the European cause foward on two key assumptions: first that, under the direction of the FO, Britain would become the arbiter of Europe; and secondly, argued Evans, that

> the supra-national element in the Treaty of Rome could be safely ignored wherever and whenever the FO deemed that it seriously infringed on traditional British constitutional rights. There was no reason, in the eyes of the FO, why Britain's essential sovereignty need be impaired.[16]

Meanwhile two powerful pro-Europe top civil servants held sway at the Treasury: Sir Frank Lee, Permanent Secretary, and Sir William Armstrong, a fellow Permanent Secretary who later became head of the Civil Service. Together these seven came to stamp a European consciousness on Britain and to deliver powerful support for the European cause.

The views of the Foreign Office and the Washington diplomats were particularly forceful. Growing opposition by De Gaulle to what he feared would be American domination of Europe led the Kennedy administration to push for British entry to prevent the Six being turned into a neutralist if not anti-American bloc. Macmillan, visiting America in April 1961 was told by Kennedy that the United States would be very supportive of British membership. Schlesinger recalls in his memoirs:

> Kennedy fully understood the economic difficulties British entry would bring to the United States. But these were in his mind overborne by political benefits. If Britain joined the Market, London could offset the eccentricities of policy in Paris and Bonn; moreover, Britain, with its world obligations, could keep the EEC from becoming a high-tariff, inward-looking, white man's club. Above all, with British membership, the market could become the basis for a true federation of Europe.[17]

On August 21 1961 Macmillan said he was making a formal application to the Common Market to see 'whether conditions existed in which membership might be possible' – a cover for entry on what was negotiable. Evans recalls:

> The extraordinary fact remains that the political and economic advantages have never been precisely spelled out either then or at any time since that date ... In the period 1961-63, Macmillan, Home and Heath, having been made responsible for 'Europe', were extremely guarded in what they said to British audiences; while in Brussels Heath was prepared to make declarations about Britain's commitment to a united Europe – in London there were lofty generalities and elusiveness about details.[18]

The Treasury establishment was relatively 'late on the scene' on EC membership and had been sceptical of the direct economic benefits to be enjoyed. This was largely due to the immediate and disadvantageous effect EC membership would have on British food prices which benefited from 'cheap' Commonwealth imports. The Treasury was swayed, first, by mounting problems caused by Britain's deteriorating economic performance relative to that of other countries and the appeal of an enlarged home market for British goods which the EC appeared to offer. But in this there was neither an appraisal of quite how an enlarged market was a precondition of economic success – other countries such as Japan, Canada and Hong Kong having small domestic markets – or of how the switch from Commonwealth raw material and food imports to European finished and semi-finished goods which were near substitutes for Britain's products, would be of benefit.

Sir Frank Lee's belief that Britain would benefit from the cold shower of competition became accepted dogma. Meanwhile the Foreign Office continued to feed in favourable reports on the Common Market into the Whitehall and political machines consistently through the 1960s. This was augmented by a propaganda drive funded from outside Britain, the scale of which was without precedent: between 1960 and 1970 the European Commission Information Service spent some £10 million in a campaign specifically targeted at MPs, business-men, opinion formers and the Press. Critics were isolated and marginalised.

Britain's application for membership was twice vetoed by De Gaulle. But these rejections only seemed to enhance the myth that entry of itself would lead to a renaissance of the British economy. It was seized upon as such by the Wilson administra-tion after the July 1966 economic crisis. Wilson's biographer Ben Pimlott noted:

> After the July crisis, in Roy Jenkins' words, Wilson 'required constant bounce to get back'. The Common Market option, in this context, looked like a trampoline. If there was also a sense in which (as Hugh Cudlipp of the pro-Market *Mirror* put it) Wilson's discovery of Europe was a gigantic attempt 'to distract attention from Rhodesia and the economic mess at home' it was also a perfectly reasonable bid to revive the Government's flagging spirit.[19]

De Gaulle would have none of it, telling Wilson that entry had to be earned, Britain and its people 'should on their own behalf and for themselves achieve a profound economic and political transformation', and that Britain also needed to dem-onstrate independence from the United States (he correctly foretold the disaster awaiting America over Vietnam).

During the debate over membership in the early 1970s the Conservative prime minister Edward Heath gave assurances that the decision to enter would require not just consent but 'the full-hearted consent of Parliament and people'. Here was a formidable challenge for the elite. In 1971 opinion polls showed 60 to 65 per cent opposed to entry. In March 1971 Opinion Research Centre summarised the views of people questioned on the issue:

> There is a conspiracy on the part of politicians, media owners and

big business to commit Britain to joining the Common Market before the public has had any chance to appraise the pros and cons or to know precisely what is happening. They are confronted with an unusual agreement between all three political parties that Britain should join, so normal political allegiances give them no guidance. They tend to feel that they are fed only the information that is favourable to Britain joining.[20]

How, then, was 'full-hearted consent' to be achieved? The European Community Information Service embarked on a £1 million a year education programme on the virtues of membership. This was augmented by a £250,000 public relations and advertising campaign by the European Movement. It held 4,000 meetings attended by 100,000 people and despatched vast quantities of literature. It sent out 290,000 reply-paid envelopes expressing support for Britain's entry which people were invited to return (only 6,000 did so). Some 1.5 million copies of the British European newspaper were printed and 6.5 million items of literature distributed. The voices against entry struggled under this cataract of pro-market propaganda.

For the Labour Party, membership of the EC was a continual source of division. Wilson sought to bridge the divide by seeking a renegotiation of the terms of entry. James Callaghan, who led the 'renegotiations', believed that membership would not alter a fundamental truth of Britain's predicament:

> I shared neither the conviction of the pro-marketeers that it would result in a vast improvement in our economic performance nor the deep despair of the anti-marketeers that membership would ruin Britain. I continued to affirm publicly and privately … that Britain's economic salvation depended on ourselves; whether we were in or out of the Community was marginal to the result.[21]

A contributory factor in the collapse of the Heath government at the February 1974 general election was the intervention of Enoch Powell on the Common Market issue and his call to supporters to vote Labour on the grounds that it was the only party offering a reconsideration of membership. Heath, he argued, had only been given a mandate to explore the terms of membership, not to sign Britain up for membership. He told a huge meeting in the Bull Ring, Birmingham, which drew 2,000:

The House of Commons was never given a hint that any such commitment was going to be undertaken, nor afterwards was it ever invited to debate, still less approve it ... Never was the full-hearted consent of Parliament and people more conspicuously absent than when Britain was hi-jacked into the EEC.

In the 1975 Referendum, the array of forces and the resources deployed by the European Movement and the Common Market institutions left only the margin of victory in doubt. The three main parties campaigned for a Yes vote as did the business and City establishments and virtually the entire national press. The European Movement, its coffers boosted by government grants and a sum of £800,000 from three anonymous donors, one of them thought to be a United States government agency, embarked on one of the most expensive political campaigns ever mounted in Britain. Brian Kingham, a Conservative Euro-enthusiast at the time, recalled: 'Money was no object for the Yes campaign. The impression given was that if any was needed, a phone call to Buckingham Gate (the London headquarters of the European Movement) would bring round all you required in a van.'

During the campaign the pro-Common Market alliance spent £1.8 million. Against this the £133,000 spent by the anti market groups stood little chance. 'Full-hearted support' of the British people, leveraged by the expenditure of £13 against each £1 spent on the arguments against entry, clearly required some cajoling. Given such a deployment of promotional and propaganda firepower, the combined efforts of three party machines and the business and corporate lobbies, it was a surprise only that more than a third of the electorate chose not to vote, and almost nine million of those who did voted No.

Far from Britain's twice rebuffed membership progressing from some remorseless tide of popular will, it sprang from the traumatic faultline of Suez, the ensuing failure of self-confidence, doubts about Britain's ability to survive as an independent country, and the requirements of American economic expansionism and Cold War diplomacy. The European unity agenda has never been accepted by the people of Britain and its justification in economic terms never proved. Nor were doubts and opposition to the EC and its unity agenda in any sense marginal: they came to be expressed by six out of ten post-war prime ministers.

More fundamentally, in joining the EC Britain exchanged a global vision for a regional one. It took the amiable and avuncular Lord Whitelaw, for so long the invisible guiding hand of the Conservative Party, to stumble out the truth: 'I don't think the hearts of the British people are ever really quite in Europe.'

Notes

1. Quoted by Robert Skidelsky in *Interests and Obsessions*, 1993, ch. 51, p. 340.

2. Churchill, *Post-War Speeches*, vols I-III.

3. Ernest Bevin to the House of Commons, November 29 1950.

4. Lord Avon, *Full Circle*, p. 29.

5. Stephen George, *Britain and European Integration since 1945*, 1991, p. 5.

6. Quoted by Douglas Evans in *While Britain Slept: The Selling of the Common Market*, 1975, p. 14.

7. George, op. cit., ch. 2, p. 40.

8. Churchill to the House of Commons, May 11 1953.

9. Rab Butler, *The Art of the Possible*, 1971.

10. Hugh Thomas, *The Suez Affair*, 1966.

11. See Alan Sked and Chris Cook, *Post War Britain: A Political History, 1945-1992*, 1993, ch. 5, pp. 136-7.

12. Martin Wight, quoted in Robert Skidelsky and Victor Bogdanov (eds) *The Age of Affluence*, 1970, and reprinted in Skidelsky's *Interests and Obsessions*, ch. 48, p. 318.

13. Quoted by Sked & Cook, op. cit., ch. 5, p. 136.

14. Skidelsky, op. cit., pp. 316-17.

15. Evans, op. cit., p. 23.

16. Ibid., p. 90.

17. Arthur Sclesinger, *A Thousand Days: John F. Kennedy in the White House*, 1965, p. 720.

18. Evans, op. cit., pp. 28 and 29-30.

19. Ben Pimlott, *Harold Wilson*, 1992, p. 435.

20. Quoted by Patrick Cosgrave in *The Lives of Enoch Powell*, 1989.

21. James Callaghan, *Time and Chance*, 1987.

On the Euro-ratchet

The Community is no federation of provinces or counties. It constitutes a Community of great and established nations, each with its own personality and traditions ... There is no question of any erosion of essential national sovereignty. All the countries concerned recognise that an attempt to impose a majority view in a case where one or more members consider their vital national interests to be at stake should imperil the very fabric of the Community.

White Paper on the UK and European Community,
July 1971 HMSO CMND 4715

The relevant fact about the history of the British Isles and above all of England is its separateness in a political sense from the history of continental Europe. The English have never belonged and have always known that they did not belong to it ... Above all, we have no written constitution, the unrestricted sovereignty of parliament is the ultimate guarantee of our freedom, both collectively and individually: if the words could ever be used 'Parliament must do this' or 'Parliament cannot do this', it would be the sign, and would be understood to be the sign, that both our liberties and our independence had lost their guarantee.

Enoch Powell MP, Brussels, January 1972

Throughout the 1980s Whitehall's Euro-establishment sought to draw Britain closer to the economies of Europe. But of a meeting of hearts and minds there was little sign. Indeed, as the politics of European convergence gathered momentum, there was widespread antipathy and resistance in Britain, led by Prime Minister Margaret Thatcher. This division over Britain's relationship with Europe, evident in substance as it was in tone, reached not only to the heart of economic and monetary policy but also to Britain's definition of herself and her place in the world.

In one extraordinary period, beginning with the Delors plan for economic and monetary union, Europe was to bring about the resignation of Britain's Trade and Industry Secretary

(Nicholas Ridley); the demotion and resignation of the Foreign
Secretary (Sir Geoffrey Howe); the resignation of the Chancellor
(Nigel Lawson); the resignation of the Prime Minister's chief
economic adviser (Sir Alan Walters) and the downfall of Margaret Thatcher herself.

The outstanding characteristic of the period of Mrs
Thatcher's prime ministership was the absorption and approval
of the laws and practices of an external institution that was
without precedent in Britain. So great was the volume of EC
legislation that special fast-track procedures were introduced
by Parliament to cope with 'harmonisation'. This period also saw
Britain's signing of the 1986 Single European Act which introduced European majority vote over domestic veto in numerous
areas of Brussels legislation. This at once nullified assurances
given in the 1971 White Paper and strengthened the hand of
the European Commission.

Several characteristics of the EC were to lead directly to the
crisis of the British political class in the 1990s. The first was the
insistent push for greater powers and jurisdiction for European
institutions. The second was the continuing push for economic
and monetary convergence. And the third was the constant
promulgation of the myth that economic growth would inevitably come – indeed, could only come – from European convergence. However, the most striking characteristic was the way
European convergence proceeded by way of ratchet advance,
which turned doubters and sceptics into active participants.
There was a relentless accretion of power and decision-making
to European institutions, ranging from the European Commission and the European Parliament to the European Court of
Justice. Proposals to introduce new supra-national institutions
or functions would be made. Britain, uncomfortable with them
would then offer counter proposals which modified the original,
but all the time the supra-national process was being advanced
by a net accrual: 'two steps forward, one step back', to reverse
the dictum of Lenin.

The vision of ever-growing union could be traced to the Treaty
of Rome. It was to receive a powerful re-enervating impulse from
the European politics of the 1980s. Margaret Thatcher was to
develop deep misgivings about the federal ambitions of the EC.
She felt ill at ease with its socialistic and bureaucratic approach
to matters of trade, agriculture and business, and in particular

with its implicit anti-Americanism and regionalist view of the world.

But to what degree were her objections shared by fellow-members of her government? And how far were they representative of the broad feelings of the British people? These questions are posed by some of the accounts of Britain's relations with the EC over this time. The prevailing version is that of an abrasive, insistent, often tiresome woman – 'That woman!' – against the reasoned and sophisticated diplomats and leaders of Europe: cool heads subjected to an intransigent and belligerent hectoring. In the context of European policy this abrasiveness reflected not only her own personality and manner but her agnosticism about Europe – 'a non-believer who still went to church' was one description. Here was not a combativeness of pose for effect. It came – and this was, perhaps, her greatest crime in the eyes of the continentalists – from a conjunction of heart and mind.

But from where else did it spring? The tendency of commentators to personalise this period of Britain's relations with Europe, to present it as a series of gladiatorial skirmishes between an isolated Thatcher on the one side and a brow-beaten EC on the other, disguises the extent to which her stance was now endorsed by some senior departments of government, especially the Treasury. But most troubling of all, it misses 'the elephant in the room' of our history – the very heart of the British mood at this time. Throughout this period Mrs Thatcher was to prove more in step with the changing tide of public opinion in Britain, both over Britain's contributions to the Community budget and the impetus to a federalist Europe. No British Prime Minister can long pursue a policy against the grain of the prevailing public mood, and Mrs Thatcher's premiership was the longest sustained tenure of this office since Lord Salisbury's.

How could this have been achieved by the isolated, inflexible, belligerent and tedious woman of historical account? Setting aside the constitutional limits to which the British executive could pursue a policy of acquiescent subordination to the federalist thrust of the EC, and the limits imposed by the markets on politically determined exchange-rate convergence, the sanction of public feeling in Britain was running counter to the direction in which EC orthodoxy was pulling.

The first major battle in European relations was over Britain's contribution to the Community budget. This was particularly embarrassing for the continentalists since it was on the economic benefits that membership was sold to the voters. By 1979 it became clear that Britain's contribution was to exceed £1 billion. What triggered the row was not the absolute amount but the size of Britain's contribution relative to that of other EC countries. Britain was receiving only a tenth of EC spending on agriculture (which accounted for two-thirds of the total budget) while contributing a fifth of total revenue. Although seventh in terms of GDP per head, she was, with Germany, the largest net contributor to the budget.

First warnings of trouble came in a speech by Mrs Thatcher at Strasbourg in November 1979 where she declared that

> Britain cannot accept the present situation on the budget. It is demonstrably unjust. It is politically indefensible. I cannot play Sister Bountiful to the Community while my own electorate are being asked to forgo improvements in the fields of health, education, welfare and the rest.[1]

The battle erupted at the EC summit in Dublin later that month. For French President Valéry Giscard d'Estaing and German Chancellor Helmut Schmidt, Mrs Thatcher's intervention struck as a rude intrusion into the lofty-ceilinged drawing-rooms of the Paris-Bonn axis where they had just drawn up a grand plan for economic and monetary union and sat as key-holders of a new European destiny. France and Germany thought the 1975 referendum had settled the question of Britain's terms of entry and were reluctant to concede a third negotiation on Britain's budget contribution. Britain, in their view, had asked to join Le Club and was thus obliged to stick by the rules. But in demanding 'Britain's own money back' the Prime Minister enjoyed the support of the Treasury and its senior ministers who also shared her misgivings about the extent to which the Foreign Office was prepared to fight Britain's case.

It was Nigel Lawson, then Treasury Chief Secretary, who told the Commons that Britain's contributions were 'manifestly and massively inequitable'. The extent to which the Treasury endorsed Mrs Thatcher's approach is evident in Lawson's memoirs:

The Foreign Office, however, was unhelpful and defeatist. Peter Carrington (Foreign Secretary) went so far as to tell the French that 'the net contribution problem was ultimately of our own making in the sense that we were not running our economy properly'. Fortunately, it was an issue on which Downing Street rather than the Foreign Office, led ...[2]

According to Lawson's account it was evident to the British team that one effective sanction would be to withhold our contributions to the budget. In conditions of tight secrecy Treasury officials and law officers were asked to draft a Parliamentary Bill to provide the legal backing for such a move. Lawson recalls: 'The Bill was never published, let alone introduced. But we discreetly let it be known that the issue of withdrawal was being considered.'[3] 'Indiscreetly' might have been the more accurate word. At meetings in Luxembourg and Brussels the following spring rebates were negotiated for 1980 and 1981 worth £1.6 billion. A third rebate of £476 million was later secured. And at the EC summit in Fontainebleau in 1984 Britain secured a further rebate and an automatic formula for refunds in subsequent years. The rebate total came to £2.5 billion, equivalent to 65 per cent of Britain's contributions.

But the settlement did not staunch the growing misgivings many in Britain were now expressing about the EC. Its ever-growing bureaucracy and obsessive concern to regulate and harmonise the last detail of service or product from the content of sausages to the shape of cucumbers was a fertile source of ridicule in the press. Far from integration with Europe providing a galvanising purpose and spur to free trade and business confidence there was indifference and doubt. The most telling measure of the national mood was the turn-out for the elections of British representatives to the European Parliament. Here was an opportunity for Britain's enthusiasm for the EC and support for its role as a fully integrated European player to be endorsed by popular vote.

A huge information and persuasion campaign was launched to explain the work of the European Parliament, the importance of Britain's voice in Europe and its function as a check on the bureaucracy. A high turn-out would also legitimise the standing of the European Parliament: indeed such an endorsement by the oldest Parliamentary democracy in the world would strengthen its hand in dealings with the European Commission and the Council of Ministers.

Far from providing such an endorsement, the elections were to prove a telling measure of the gulf that had opened up between the political elite and the British people. Huge Euro-constituencies were created, throwing together large areas of Britain in an arbitrary and alien way that made no sense to their 750,000 or so voters per constituency.

The first election in 1979 for British representatives to the European Parliament attracted less than 40 per cent of the electorate. It was hoped that, as the reality of Britain's EC membership sank home and the volume of legislation testified to the importance of what was happening in Brussels, the interest would increase. But instead, by 1984, the turn-out was just 32.4 per cent. By 1989, as Britain approached the Single Market and democratic endorsement of the EC was more imperative than ever, it was 34.2 per cent. These figures were damning for the European movement and in particular for the Whitehall Euro-elite. It was one thing to say that Britain had voted to join the EC. It was another to argue that the electorate had, on any of the three occasions it had an opportunity to do so, endorsed and legitimised such a profound change.

Mrs Thatcher, far from being isolated and alone, was articulating a cool and sceptical view in the country at large in expressing doubts not only about the inefficiencies of the Common Agricultural Policy but about the supra-national ambitions of the EC. Her animosity was not directed against greater trade and business with the EC. Of that she approved, and she encouraged it. It was directed against a federalist vision of Europe.

But the pressure to conform was to intensify. In June 1983 the EC heads of state signed a 'solemn declaration on European Union' – the Genscher-Colombo plan – urging more co-operation between European institutions. A Government White Paper in 1984, *Europe – The Future*, called for the completion of the single market. It set out a way ahead for the EC which avoided the federalist pretensions of Brussels but was positive in tone. But the federalist agenda rolled on. After the 1983 Stuttgart call for a 'relaunch' of the EC, the European Parliament adopted by 321 votes to 31 a draft treaty for European union championed by the veteran Italian federalist Altiero Spenelli. In June 1985 the

Milan European Council agreed to an inter-governmental conference to revise the Treaty of Rome which would give increased powers to the European Parliament, abolish national voting and introduce majority voting on a large number of issues.

The alternative championed by Britain was the Single European Act which sought a level common market by 1992, in which harmonisation ran rampant. The SEA was a classic example of the European ratchet in action. It was supported by Britain as an alternative to the sweeping Spenelli plan. But it bore Europe further down the road of political integration than when the process started, and further than the British government realised or intended.

Mrs Thatcher was later to claim that she was misled by the Foreign Office. In any event, her endorsement of the Act was less for any advance it made than for the advance it prevented. She told the Commons: 'It does not change anything. If it did I would not have signed it ... . There is no erosion of national sovereignty.' But the Act altered the balance of power within the Community by giving enhanced decision-making functions to the European Parliament and introducing qualified majority voting in certain areas. These changes made it difficult for a member country to block Community business – a vital safeguard of our national interests frequently invoked in the 1975 referendum to allay fears over British sovereignty. It expanded the bailiwick of the European Parliament (into environmental matters and health and safety at work) and it vastly augmented the scope of the European Court of Justice to impose federalising measures. The most important doctrine that the Court of Justice established is that Community law must always take precedence over national law where there is a conflict – a direct challenge to the sovereignty of Parliament.

EC directives were by now swamping the Commons, and measures reaching into every facet of British life were being nodded through a House unable to cope with the scrutiny and consideration required. The EC Select Committee on European Secondary Legislation in its report for 1985-86 expressed concern that Parliament had been given no opportunity to comment on the provisions of the SEA before its being agreed by heads of government. It was not the last time that parliaments and people would be steam-rollered in this way.

Later, in 1988, European Commission President Jacques

Delors confidently predicted that within ten years 80 per cent
of economic legislation would be directed from the Community.
Outside the Foreign Office, the Euro-elite and the main political
parties there was little support, either for the type of legislation
that Delors envisaged or the institutional framework required
to enforce it. But among the continentalists in the Conservative
Party there was increasing irritation at the combativeness of
the Prime Minister's style, which was fostering, in their eyes, a
negative image of EC institutions and 'upsetting our European
partners'. The Treasury, now under Lawson, was pushing ever
harder for Britain's membership of the Exchange Rate Mechanism. But Lawson's support for the ERM was never based on
a rosy view of the prospects of economic convergence in the
Community.

Nor was it powered by a vision of European economic and
monetary union. Rather, it sprang at first from a domestic
political consideration, and a fear that, when it came to the test,
even his Cabinet colleagues would opt to relax domestic monetary discipline to avoid political unpopularity and the risk of
electoral defeat. The ERM offered an external means of bearing
down on inflation. But in Lawson's view it was just those who
would be likely to 'wobble' on inflation who would be likely to
prove the most enthusiastic to join the ERM. Thatcher, inde-
pendently advised by the economist Sir Alan Walters, had held
out against ERM membership, keeping pressure from the Foreign Office and the Treasury at bay with a commitment to join
but only 'when the time is ripe'.

In June 1988 came a development that would have major
consequences for Britain and for Europe. Jacques Delors was
charged by the Hanover summit with setting up a working party
on economic and monetary union and to propose steps towards
such union – the forerunner of the Maastricht Treaty. In September he received a standing ovation for a speech to the TUC
annual conference calling for a 'social dimension' to the Single
Market. It helped swing the Labour Party round to enthusiastic
endorsement of the programme for economic and monetary
union.

Thatcher, infuriated by Delors, and already determined to
pre-empt his report, replied in a landmark speech at Bruges in
Belgium later that month. It challenged the Delors vision of
Europe on three fronts. First, it attacked the development of a

socialist EC. Secondly, it championed the cause of the newly
liberated countries of Eastern Europe, urging that the Community be enlarged to accept them. And thirdly, it emphasised the
need for the EC to develop as a free trade area and move away
from bureaucratic regulation and controls. The speech also had
a strong international dimension that tended to be overlooked
in press reports. It was a reminder to Britain that while continental Europe would always be a vital trading area, Britain had
a world perspective which must not be blocked out by the cause
of European regionalism.

The speech was a watershed in Britain's relations with
Europe. It offered a markedly different vision of the future of
the Community. More immediately, it brought to the fore a split
in the government over Britain's approach to the convergence
programme. It doing so it marked the beginning of the end of
her premiership.

The Bruges speech struck a chord with many in Britain and
particularly in the ranks of the government's supporters. Early
the following year the Bruges Group was formed. Its principal
moving spirit was Lord Harris of High Cross, founder of the
influential Institute of Economic Affairs. The group attracted a
clutch of eminent academics – Norman Stone, Patrick Minford,
Roger Scruton, Tim Congdon, Martin Holmes, Adam Zamoyski
and Alan Sked, who later went on to found the Anti-Federalist
League. The group was backed by many leading business figures including Lord White of the Hanson group, Sir James
Goldsmith, Grand Metropolitan chief Allen Sheppard, David
Peake of Kleinwort Benson, Trusthouse Forte head Rocco Forte,
BP chief Sir Peter Walters, Sir Ian MacGregor, Garfield Weston
of Associated British Foods and Lord Pennock. Early meetings
of the group at the Reform Club booked for an audience of 50
found 250 or more queueing at the door.

The Delors Report was published in the spring of 1989. It
envisaged three stages: first, the completion of the single market and all countries participating in the ERM; second, the
machinery to effect a common economic policy and a European
central bank to manage the single currency; and third, the fixing
of exchange rates, with machinery for paying infrastructure
grants to poorly performing economies to create uniform economic performance throughout the EC.

The Report also argued that the decision to enter the first

stage would be a decision to embark on the entire process. Chancellor Nigel Lawson and the Treasury opposed the single currency proposals from the first. Others in the Cabinet were cool towards the proposals for Stages Two and Three. The Report as a whole would effectively strip member countries of discretion over interest rates and exchange-rate and monetary policy and give European institutions all the main levers of economic power. For a Conservative government the rationale behind regional infrastructure grants was deeply questionable, as its leverage effect on regional growth rates in Britain could never overcome factors of geography, skill-base and location. The most fundamental objection, shared across the Cabinet, was that without underlying economic convergence the whole Delors vision was flawed. In the event the re-unification of Germany and the ensuing inflation and sharply rising federal-government deficit was to undermine the ambitious timetables for currency union.

But even had the Cabinet been more sympathetic there was an additional problem: the Delors Report would have to be accepted by the whole of the House of Commons. The only department that wanted to keep the door open was the Foreign Office. Ridley recalls:

> To implement the Delors Report would require a new treaty, and that ... also required legislation: the House of Commons had the power to reject it and would certainly have voted against it. That seemed to me, and probably to Margaret Thatcher, to be the right reaction. The Foreign Office influence, however, kept pressing for us to put forward an alternative suggestion, a counter proposal, that would at least keep us present in the negotiations and thus not jeopardise our good European 'credentials'.[4]

Unable, or unwilling, to press our European 'credentials' over the ERM in Cabinet, Lawson and Howe decided to confront Mrs Thatcher in private. Immediately before the EC summit in Madrid in June 1989 – in an incident that became known as the 'Madrid ambush' – they threatened to resign unless she gave a specific commitment to join the ERM.

Here again the Euro-ratchet was at work. Lawson in his memoirs recalls that the reason for his stand with Howe was that unless Britain joined the ERM she would have no influence on the discussions over EMU. Mrs Thatcher, reluctantly, and on conditions, agreed. But the affair deeply troubled her, since she felt she was being pushed down the convergence road against her will. In July she moved Howe from the Foreign Office to be leader of the House of Commons, a demotion that was to breed a fatal rancour.

In October 1989 Lawson resigned as Chancellor, citing his opposition to the reappointment of Sir Alan Walters as the Prime Minister's economic adviser. By this time the economy was in serious trouble: the inevitable result, as critics saw it, of the Lawson policy of putting the exchange rate before domestic monetary conditions. Lawson was succeeded by John Major.

In the summer of 1990 Mrs Thatcher was to lose another member of her Cabinet over Europe – Trade and Industry Secretary Nicholas Ridley, who resigned after outspoken remarks on Germany and Europe in an interview in the *Spectator*.

As was to happen repeatedly, Foreign Office claims of 'influence' resulting from collaboration failed to materialise. At a European Council meeting in Rome in October 1990 the pace of EMU, far from being slackened, was accelerated, with a starting date of 1994 advanced for the Delors plan. Later that month Mrs Thatcher tore into the federalist programme in the Commons: 'Mr Delors said ... he wanted the European Parliament to be the democratic body of the Community. He wanted the Commission to be the Executive, and he wanted the Council of Ministers to be the senate. No, no, no.'[5] The Euro-fanatics were appalled. In November Sir Geoffrey Howe resigned as Leader of the Commons, delivering a bruising speech that sparked the Conservative coup that led to Mrs Thatcher's downfall. The happiest man in Europe was Jacques Delors.

The division over Europe in the Conservative Party was to polarise dramatically on the removal of Mrs Thatcher. There were two lines of 'apostolic succession' and the clash divided the country. Supporters of Thatcher could claim that she was the latest in a line running from Churchill, through Eden, Powell and the radical, free-enterprise Right. This line regarded the nurturing of a national consciousness and self-confidence as the highest purpose in politics. The pro-European apostolic line ran from Macmillan, through Heath and Whitelaw to Howe and Hurd. It saw in Thatcher an interloper, an aberration against a more enduring tradition of Conservatism which put amelioration and pragmatism before grand vision and policy. Her growing hostility to Europe and in particular the tone of that 'No, no, no' in the Commons caused her removal from office, restored the 'true' line and buffed up Britain's Euro-credentials. But which line was the true Conservative succession? And which the pretender?

In the event, the party chose as successor one who offered a bridge between the two: a Thatcherite disciple but with a softer tone on Europe. The new Prime Minister was a little-known, inexperienced and self-effacing but popular minister: John Major.

Neither the negative qualities ascribed to Mrs Thatcher nor her underlying political disposition had resulted in a brief Prime Ministership. On the contrary, her stance on Europe should be seen as a contributory factor to her extraordinary length of tenure. It was by virtue of the position she took, first on Britain's budgetary contributions, subsequently on the timing of Britain's entry into the European ERM, and later on her questioning of the drive towards federalism, that she remained to the last the most respected and formidable British Prime Minister since Churchill.

It was not unpopularity at the grass roots which forced the resignation issue but a revolt of the Conservative Euro-elite. Left to the broad mass of Conservative supporters in the country, she would never have been forced from office in the way she was. Moreover it has to be questioned whether even a dedicated pro-European would not have been embroiled in the difficulties that were finally to ensnare Mrs Thatcher and ultimately bring about the coup against her. Prime Ministers are appointed to safeguard Britain's national interests in dealings with other countries and to make these interests secure, compatible with the requirements of economic and political stability.

There is a further obligation to work within the constraints of public opinion and the wishes of Parliament. But Britain found herself the victim of a European ratchet against which she resisted in vain. She stood little chance against the combined power of continental leaders. She stood even less chance as a result of a fifth column at home, a visionless political elite without whose unstinting, determined and dogmatic desire to be 'at the heart of Europe', the ratchet could never have turned.

Notes

1. Speech to the European Council at Strasbourg, June 21-22 1979.
2. Nigel Lawson, *Memoirs of a Radical*, 1992, ch.10, p. 109.
3. Ibid., p. 110.
4. Nicholas Ridley, *My Style of Government*, 1991, p. 149.
5. Margaret Thatcher speaking in the Commons, October 30 1990.

6

Game, Set and Maastricht

The transfer by the States from their domestic legal system to the Community legal system of the rights and obligations arising from under the Treaty carries with it a permanent limitation of their sovereign rights, against which a subsequent unilateral act incompatible with the concept of the Community cannot prevail.
European Court of Justice, Costa v. ENEL

This Treaty marks a new stage in the process of creating an ever closer union among the peoples of Europe ...
Article A, Treaty on European Union

The parts of the treaty dealing with political union are just as important as those concerning economic and monetary union ... An economic union will survive only if it is based on a political union.
Chancellor Helmut Kohl, *Financial Times*, January 4 1993

Now we've signed it – we had better read it!
Douglas Hurd, February 7 1992

No event more marked the exhaustion of the British political elite, its bankruptcy of global vision and ideal, than Britain's endorsement of the Treaty on European Union. For all the intensity of debate among the few who had struggled to read its 306 pages, 17 protocols and 33 declarations, it was a private enthusiasm. The mood in the country was one of fatigue. 'Maastricht' became a dreaded word, a crowd-disperser at a hundred yards.

For the Foreign Office this was arguably the best response it could have hoped for, since its apologies for the Treaty did not stand up to scrutiny. It could barely disguise the failed assumptions and ideas that had nurtured the pro-Europeans for a generation. The reality of European convergence brought together the sense of British national decline with inevitable surrender of will, and at Maastricht the lines crossed.

This was no sudden crisis or confrontation for Britain but the culmination of a slow corrosion of her economic, legal and parliamentary sovereignty. After the otherthrow of Mrs Thatcher the continentalists hoped that relations with Europe would take a more positive and pro-active turn. That hope lay in the personality of John Major. Here was a man of disarming charm, the soft face of Thatcherism, agreeable to the voters but a Cabinet stalwart whom Thatcherite loyalists somehow felt was 'one of us'. He was unknown, untested and an enigma.

But it was on the premise of his being 'one of us', offered by a brief Chancellorship and even briefer role as Foreign Secretary, that the Conservative Party and in particular its Right wing rallied round the new Prime Minister. What did it matter that he was the son of a trapeze artist or garden-gnome manufacturer? Or a failed applicant as a bus conductor? Or a man curiously unsure about his academic qualifications? Were not these the very attributes that gave him political appeal and brought needed colour to an otherwise grey image?

It was this lack of curiosity about his past that gave John Major the premiership. He stood in high regard for being housing chairman of Lambeth Council, but contemporaries remembered him less as a radical lionheart than as a spender. Nor, in his City or parliamentary career, had he carved out a position of distinction. As early as 1981 he had spoken in favour of a European exchange rate system and by 1989 he was an enthusiast. He supported the Foreign Office line that it was necessary for Britain to join the ERM in order to influence the discussions of the European Council at Strasbourg on European economic and monetary union. As Britain's economy entered recession he supported the European convergence process. At the Rome meeting of the European Council in December 1990 he was warmly received while British attitudes made a fuller adjustment to the realities of European union. Some were less gracious. Jacques Delors put his own marker down on Britain's future with the remark that since he had arranged one crisis (that of the downfall of Mrs Thatcher the previous month, taking sinister credit for her overthrow) he could always arrange another.

In 1990 Major, then Chancellor, helped push for Britain's ERM entry throughout that year. He originally wanted the pound to join the ERM in July 1990, less out of the disciplinary effects it would have on domestic money supply than that it would coincide with the decision of the French and Italians to abolish exchange controls. ERM entry was hailed for its dual effect: that it would re-establish Britain's 'good European' credentials and that it would bear down on inflation to make Britain one of the lowest-inflation countries in Europe. Almost the entire business and financial establishment, the CBI and the financial press, the *Economist* and the *Financial Times* in particular, applauded the move.

By February 1991 a group of economists dubbed the Liverpool Six (after their moving spirit, Professor Patrick Minford of Liverpool University) and including Professor Tim Congdon and Bill Martin of UBS, wrote to *The Times* predicting 'real disaster' unless Britain left the ERM or devalued within the system. As the year progressed, bankruptcies soared and tens of thousands of home-owners began to fall behind in their mortgage repayments as the high-interest-rate regime, far from proving temporary, extended into the autumn and on into the late summer of 1992.

Gradually the consensus behind the ERM policy began to crumble. The high-interest-rate regime moved to the centre stage throughout 1992. Business failures and home repossessions increased. Less visible, but of huge implication, was the collapse of the public finances. With the recession, tax receipts fell and spending on unemployment and welfare rose. This was exacerbated by higher departmental spending by ministers and a generally more lenient climate on public expenditure following the departure of Mrs Thatcher. Between the autumn of 1991 and January the following year, Treasury estimates of the PSBR rocketed from £28 billion to £35 billion. So much for the 'discipline' of the ERM.

Meanwhile Major's 'charm offensive' proved ineffective against the Paris/Bonn axis and the engine of European convergence. The Kohl-Mitterrand friendship stood as a bulwark against any attempt to reform the Common Agricultural Policy – the very 'inside' influence that the Foreign Office claimed increasing British collaboration with Europe would bring. The Luxembourg summit in July 1991 resulted in a Draft Treaty on European Union, envisaging, *inter alia*, political and monetary union, common health and employment provisions (the Social

Chapter), common European citizenship and a 'federal voca-
tion'. It went forward to the little town of Maastricht.

British public opinion did not go with it. Opinion polls at the
time showed 55 per cent against monetary union and 53 per cent
against political union. Analysed in terms of political support,
75 per cent of Conservative voters, 66 per cent of Liberal and 55
per cent of Labour were against giving more power to Brussels.
But Major's response was that Britain had no choice but to
remain 'at the heart of Europe'. Seldom had a measure with
such profound constitutional consequences been presented to
the electorate with such backtracking dissemblage. The government's public relations approach was the giveway: it hailed the
negotiated opt-outs, not the substantive Treaty.

What was also notable was the contrast between the selling
of Common Market membership in the early 1970s and the
approach to Maastricht. Gone was the confident, enthusiastic
'Hail, new dawn' rhetoric. The argument now was: 'We are lucky
to get this. The alternative would be worse.' It was later to
change to: 'Vote for this, because it will never work.'

In tone and content Maastricht marked a quantum leap in
the process of integration. By Article A the signatories 'establish
among themselves a European Union'. In the preamble the
signatories declare themselves 'resolved to establish a citizenship common to nationals of their countries'. Article G(C) estab-
lishes 'citizenship of the Union' and alters the name of the
'European Economic Community' to 'European Community',
thus at a stroke removing the key apologia for UK membership
– that its purpose was solely, or primarily, economic.

At the heart of the Treaty was the provision for the establishment of a European Central Bank and a single currency to
be attained in three stages. The economic policies of the member
states were now to be regarded 'as a matter of common concern',
and signatories were to obey 'broad guidelines of the economic
policies of the member states'. A system of 'multilateral surveil-
lance' was established to monitor this concern.

In other areas the powers and jurisdiction of the Community
institutions were advanced. In addition to proposals which
would remove the right of member states to operate their own
immigration and asylum policies, there was the establishment
of a common foreign and defence policy, the establishment of an

economic and social cohesion fund, and the extended use of qualified majority voting in the Council of Ministers.*

A central pillar of the Treaty is the doctrine of 'subsidiarity', the obligation to devolve power to the lowest level. Not only did this implicitly confirm the existence of an overriding supranational authority, but under the Treaty it is this authority that will decide what functions should be devolved to lower levels.

The government constantly sought to downplay the importance of the Treaty for domestic audiences. The preamble, we were assured, was 'Euro-waffle', meaning 'nothing'. Against this, President Mitterrand declared that the Treaty on European Union was even more fundamental and more far-reaching than the Treaty of Rome: its every generalisation was the stuff that mattered.

At the First Reading of the Bill to ratify the Treaty in the Commons there was only a handful of Tory rebels (Mrs Thatcher and her former Cabinet minister Nicholas Ridley abstained). But opposition on the back benches now started to grow. One reason it was slow off the ground was that getting hold of a copy of the Treaty was not easy: it was not published in Britain until after the 1992 general election, although it had been signed two months previously. The library in the Reform Club was the only place a member of the public, let alone most MPs, could procure

---

* At first sight this would appear to be a matter of no great disadvantage to Britain. But closer examination is required. Votes in the Council are distributed thus: Britain, Germany, France and Italy ten votes each; Spain, eight votes; Holland, Belgium, Portugal and Greece, five votes each; Ireland and Denmark three votes each; and Luxembourg two votes.

I am indebted to Stephen and Gill Bush for the following: A vote of 54 (out of 76) is necessary to pass a binding decision. The combined population of the seven smallest countries is 53 million and together they command 28 votes against Britain's ten with 56 million population. In the Strasbourg parliament the same seven have 134 seats against Britain's 81. Since Belgium, Holland and Luxembourg invariably vote with Germany, and Spain, France and Italy usually vote together (and also usually with Germany) Britain's disadvantage is overwhelming and makes any extension of majority voting folly. The distribution of membership in the increasingly influential Committee of the Regions has an even greater disparity between population and representation, that of the Republic of Ireland being proportionately six times that of Britain (Article 198a). (Stephen and Gill Bush, *Britain's Future, The Meaning of the Maastricht Treaty*, 1992.)

actual sight of a copy. All the main political parties, however, went into that election as enthusiastic Europeans. All were supporters of Maastricht. All were committed to our ERM membership.

Another reason why opposition was slow to grow was that Britain had been lulled by the process of continuing UK adaptation to European law. It was not in 1994 but in 1974, and not of Maastricht but of the Treaty of Rome, that Lord Denning was to liken its effect to that of 'an incoming tide. It flows into the estuaries and up the rivers. It cannot be held back.' He later returned to this metaphor and amended it: 'No longer is European law an incoming tide flowing up the estuaries of England. It is now like a tidal wave bringing down our sea walls and flowing inland over our fields and houses – to the dismay of all.'[1]

There were three areas of concern over the Treaty. One was the extension of European discretion over matters decided on by the parliaments of the member states. The second was the validity, or sea-worthiness, of Britain's negotiated opt-outs over Stage Three of economic and monetary union and especially the Social Chapter. And the third was the growing powers conferred on the European Court of Justice. Indeed much of the concern was over how much the ECJ had already become, by the time of the Treaty, the prime agency of convergence.

To understand this concern it is necessary to go back a little into the history of the Court. It is based in Luxembourg and comprises 13 judges appointed for six years. The appointments are shared out among the member states. It has a central role in the interpretation of European law. It meets *in camera*, and its proceedings do not require unanimous or even qualified majority voting as in the Council of Ministers. The oaths of appointment expressly forbid the judges to act for, or on behalf of, any member state. The appointments are made on the basis not of legal competence or experience but of 'independence' from member country judiciaries. It is a common assumption that the European Court is a neutral arbiter of disputes between the Community and the member states. It is, however, an avowedly Community institution and in its rulings and judgments seeks to advance the powers and duties of Community institutions over the individual member states. The Court's judgments have helped to accelerate the process of European integration. The Court has advanced by way of incremental revision. For example in the 1974 *van Duyn* ruling the court stated that individuals may invoke Community directives before national courts. In its 1976 ruling on the *Defrenne* case it found that the principle of equal pay for men and women laid down in Article 119 on sex equality was one of the EC's 'foundations' and so had direct effect. In the 1990 *Barber* ruling it advanced the EC's competence in pensions legislation.

The Court sees it as its duty to roll the Community forward. To effect this it draws not only upon the specifics of the Rome and Maastricht Treaties but also upon their generalities – the very ones the government claimed were without meaning. Its rulings can turn the general into the specific across wide areas of Community life. Moreover, once that competence is established it is irreversible. It is because the European Court does not rule impartially but in favour of the advancement of European integration that Britain's opt-out from the Social Chapter came to be regarded with scepticism.

Other countries would not long tolerate freedom by Britain to compete in EC markets unencumbered by Community employment and labour legislation required by the Treaty. The signatories to the Social Chapter would be able to remove Britain's competitive advantage if not by compliance then at least by partial mitigation through the European Court. Britain is already obliged under health and safety directives to comply with certain specific requirements of the Social Chapter.

The second opt-out was from Stage Three of economic and monetary union. This still left an obligation to participate in Stages One and Two. Moreover the Treaty obliges Britain to conform to certain requirements on exchange-rate and monetary policy during Stage Three even if sterling is a separate currency and opted out of the ERM.

From January 1999 the European Central Bank will issue the new single currency, replacing the currencies of the member states who satisfy the convergence criteria covering low inflation, low public-sector deficits and staying in the ERM narrow bands for at least two years without devaluation. Throughout the debates on the Treaty the government stressed the benefits of convergence, low inflation and low budget deficits in particular.

With the issue of the single currency, the national debts of all the member states will be added together and their respective central banks will hand over their central bank reserves to the European Central Bank. The recipients of EC largesse from the Cohesion Funds, such as Spain, Greece and Italy, will be supplying plenty of the former and not much of the latter.

But while these were, in the main, applauded by Conservatives as *primary* objectives, virtuous goals in themselves, in the Maastricht Treaty they are *secondary* to the goal of economic and monetary union. Further, few in the government thought to question why it was necessary for Britain to surrender its monetary sovereignty to achieve price stability, which was akin to advocating the demolition of a bank in order to thwart robbers: faultless logic, but self-defeating.

The British opt-out was questionable on three counts. First, Britain is bound, so long as it retains its own currency, to 'treat its exchange rate policy as a matter of common interest'. This obligation applies both on Stages One and Two and after the start of Stage Three to any remaining currencies, including sterling.

Secondly, Britain is required under Stages One and Two to contribute to the start-up capital and running costs of the European Monetary Institute (the forerunner of the ECB). Based on the formula for contributions, Britain would be one of the highest payers if she later decided to opt in, contributing about a fifth (i.e. about £700 million).

On the issue of ECB participation, Britain faced a Catch-22 dilemma: unless she decided to opt in, she would have no seat on the Governing Council. But if she does join, Britain's voting power in the proposed Executive Board would be 16.7 per cent of the total, and voting power in the Governing Council would be 5.6 per cent. Yet it is difficult to imagine that a British government, having participated in the preparatory work of the EMI, would 'jump off the train' the moment the EMI became the European Central Bank, forgoing any representation and influence in the decisions of a body whose deliberations would set and control exchange-rate and monetary policy throughout the Community. This has been just the argument that the government and the pro-Europeans have advanced for participation all along, and it would be out of character to abandon it at the critical moment of the institution of the ECB.

According to Martin Howe, a constitutional lawyer who has become an acknowledged expert on the Treaty, the UK's position would 'be quite invidious … . The UK would be obliged to follow ECU interest rates in order to maintain its parity, but would have no say in setting them. The UK "opt-out" from Stage Three is therefore so unattractive that it must be queried whether it is anything more than window-dressing.'[2]

Thirdly, there will be pressure on Britain to rejoin the ERM in some form and at some stage, and we would be exposed to pressure that our opting out of the ERM prejudiced the purpose of the Treaty. The Commission could bring Britain into line by taking the matter to the European Court on the grounds that Britain was persisting in pursuing an exchange-rate policy based on domestic and not EC interests.

Taken as a whole, there was barely a single clause in its 306 pages that the government actually wanted, still less that the British people had expressed a desire for. And the more MPs came to know about the Treaty, the more uncomfortable they became. In 1991-92 sterling suffered growing trouble in the ERM, and on September 16 1992, after frenzied speculative attack, it was forced out of the system. Chancellor Norman Lamont offered his resignation. Major, who had taken Britain into the ERM during his own brief Chancellorship, championed the currency convergence policy and made ERM membership the centrepiece of his economic policy, could not accept it without exposing his own position. (Major kept Lamont on, only to demand his resignation seven months later amid a deepening collapse of the Chancellor's credibility.).

Contrary to warnings from the Treasury and the Bank of England that interest rates would go even higher if Britain was not in the ERM, rates rapidly came down. A relieved Lamont revealed that he 'sang in his bath' and declared that he was now able to pursue 'a British policy in British interests'. What, one was minded to ask, had he been pursuing before?

Meanwhile Parliamentary opposition to Maastricht, boosted by a Danish referendum 'No' vote in March 1992, was growing. While subsequent referenda across Europe resulted in verdicts in favour, what deeply struck the political class was the narrowness of the victory in many cases. Of the 30.5 million people who voted in three referenda, 15.8 million were in favour of the Treaty and 14.7 million were opposed. None came closer than the referendum in France, which gave an under-whelming endorsement of just 0.75 per cent in September that year.

Against the Foreign Office and the government the Euro-rebels stood little chance of defeating the Maastricht Treaty. But they were to come astonishingly close. The Parliamentary opposition was loosely grouped round Conservative back-bencher William Cash, MP for Stafford. Cash, a Bruges Group supporter and Thatcher's former chairman of the European Committee, brought a keen legal mind to the Treaty and was soon providing an informed and incisive opposition. Other prominent opponents of Maastricht included Sir Richard Body, Peter Shore, Teddy Taylor, Teresa Gorman, Bernard Jenkin and Sir Peter Tapsell. The rebels set up a headquarters in Great College Street close to the Commons. This co-ordinated tactics, supplied research and greatly improved the effectiveness of the Parliamentary opposition which had grown to a core group of around sixty. One weakness was the failure of related groups to build a popular support movement in the country, particularly on calls for a referendum.

But gradually what seemed a minor irritation for the government came to be a nightmare. March 1993 saw a ten-day period of turmoil with the first Commons defeat of Major's premiership. Desperation and near-panic set in around the European camp. Norman Fowler, Conservative party chairman and Kenneth Clarke, then Home Secretary, strongly attacked the Maastricht rebels. Behind the scenes attempts were made to bring them into line by exerting pressure on their constituency associations. The discreet, informal pressure on the rebels was unforgiving and intense.

Also out of the limelight, the government desperately sought to do deals to secure support from minority parties. Scottish secretary Iain Lang courted the nationalists, all but guaranteeing them between six and eight seats on the Committee on the Regions in return for support. But despite all the cajoling and bullying and the efforts of the whips, the government still lost the vote on March 8 by 314 votes to 292, forcing the Bill to return to the Commons for the Report Stage. This further delayed ratification and slowed other government business to a crawl.

More drama was to come. On July 23 the government was defeated on the final vote to ratify the Treaty. Months of trench warfare came to a climax in a packed House of Commons where at least 23 Euro-rebels defied the whips. Major came close to losing an even more vital vote on a last-ditch attempt by Labour to sign Britain up to the Social Chapter. It took the casting vote of the Speaker to give the government a majority of one after the House tied 317-317. This was again after 'understandings' were reached with the minority parties, this time the Ulster Unionists.

The Prime Minister gave notice of a vote of confidence to be held the following day, backed up by a threat to call a general election if he was defeated. In effect, he told his dissenting backbenchers that if they did not vote for Maastricht with his opt-outs, they would let in Labour and get Maastricht without the opt-outs, especially from the Social Chapter. Not only did the traumas over the Bill reflect the degree to which the Conservative Party and the country were divided on Europe but also how the government's authority had ebbed. Maastricht exposed not just disarray and incompetence within the government, but a future for Britain that was dispiriting and constitutionally deeply threatening. The rebels chose to vote for a tactical loss for the time being, but it had taken a confidence motion and the threat of a general election by Major to force the Maastricht Treaty through. In the battle the rebels had exposed a fundamental vacuity and lack of ideas in Major's pro-European Cabinet.

By far the greatest, and most worrying, failing from the beginning was a lack of any questioning, either of the necessity for this Treaty or of how convergence, instead of delivering stability and growth, was de-stabilising the currency markets and pushing the continental economies deep into recession. The 'crime' lay not just in the promotion of a flawed prospectus on Europe, but promoting it in the knowledge that it was flawed. With every week that passed fresh evidence of how European uncompetitiveness, exacerbated by the Social Chapter provisions of Maastricht, was tearing into the European economies and turning the ERM into a foreign currency dealers' paradise, making its collapse a question of 'when', not 'if'.

Britain's ratification, ironically and rather appropriately, coincided with the final trauma and convulsion of the ERM. As John Major sent the official instruments of ratification, endorsed by H.M. Queen Elizabeth II, to Rome by private jet, waves of selling pressure drove the French franc through its

ERM floor. On August 1 1993, Europe was forced to recognise that convergence through a system of semi-fixed exchange rates was over. After an agreement to relax the fluctuation bands the ERM was seen to be dead in all but name and the neat Maastricht timetables for monetary union smashed to pieces.

While the economic rationale of Maastricht lay in ruins, the political rationale continued to be asserted. In fact, not only are the parts of the Treaty dealing with political union still in place, but so too are the social provisions and transfer payments to other member states. In addition Stage Two of economic and monetary union is going ahead with the establishment of the European Monetary Institute, headquartered with customary German sensitivity in the former I.G. Farben building near Frankfurt.

Sir Leon Brittan, head of European External Affairs, in a Canute-like declaration insisted: 'EMU is not going away and will not go away. The case for it is too strong. No one should underestimate the gravity of what happened at the week-end [the French franc crisis] but equally no one should under estimate the will to rebuild economic and monetary union.'

Undaunted by events, Jacques Delors confidently unveiled the latest details of the Community's economic structure plan, with £24 billion to be spent on transport and electronics infrastructure and £4 billion on common infrastructure systems. The total cost of the plan in a full year would be £33 billion, rising over five years to £100 billion.

On the constitutional front the progress of 'ever closer union' is expected to receive renewed impetus from the Treaty revision conference planned for 1996. According to the Treaty its main task is to 'maintain in full the *"acquis communautaire"* and build on it'. And it is in *acquis communautaire* that the most pernicious of the doctrines at the heart of the Community is to be found. Martin Howe, in *The Constitution After Maastricht*[3] gives this interpretation: 'The word [*acquis*] is used in the field of legal rights: *ce droit nous est acquis*, meaning "we have now established this right as ours". ... The Maastricht Treaty therefore involves an acceptance of irreversibility. Since nothing must be taken away or removed from the *"acquis communautaire"* it must forever be built on or added to.' *Acquis communautaire* will be increasingly evident in the final approach to union.

An Opinion by the European Court of Justice in December

1991[4] on the Draft Treaty on a European Economic Area (effectively bringing the EFTA countries into the EC) found, first, that the objective of all European treaties is to achieve 'concrete proposals towards European unity' and that 'free movement and competition, far from being an end in themselves are only means for attaining' this progress. It also confirmed that Community treaties 'established a new legal order for the benefit of which the states have limited their sovereign rights, in *ever wider fields*' (my emphasis).

Backed up by the ratchet effect of *acquis communautaire*, this means that an awesome and unassailable legal machine is now 'at the heart of Europe'. It is argued by some that the driving force for convergence is no longer a set of legal arrangements driven by politicians but that the legal arrangements are now being deployed to pressurise and harry recalcitrant member states.

The supreme and repeated misjudgment of the British political elite for thirty years has been to underestimate the momentum of the drive for European union. The push for European convergence since the Treaty of Rome has had a galvanising and self-renewing dynamic. For want of any rival impulse or vision, the relentless movement forges on. It feeds as much on setback as on advance, and the Treaty on European Union has been the most spectacular advance of them all.

Notes

1. Denning, Introduction to Gavin Smith, *The European Court of Justice: Judges or Policy Makers?*
2. European Court, Case 6/64, Costa v. ENEL (1964).
3. Martin Howe, *Europe and the Constitution after Maastricht*, 1992, p. 65.
4. European Court of Justice Opinion re Draft Treaty on a European Economic Area (Opinion 1/91 December 14 1991).

Good Business in Europe?

In Britain we have never quite managed to integrate the idea of
Europe into what one might call our national identity ... We see
no overriding emotional or political reason to be part of the
Community so we tend to regard each proposition which emerges
from Brussels as a discrete proposal ... We do not start from the
premise that there is a greater good being promoted by the
process of European integration, one which cannot be costed from
month to month ... .

Howard Davies, Director-General, Confederation of British
Industry, Dusseldorf, Germany, October 1993

We see the traditional EC approach to social policy as a barrier
to improved efficiency and as a job-destroying machine. In our
view, EC social programmes are based on outdated collectivist
policies geared to the rights of organised labour ... Brussels
policies give employers the incentive not to employ.

Peter Morgan, Director-General, Institute of Directors,
Haarlem, Netherlands, October 1993

Three powerful groups have provided the impulse and momentum for British integration with Europe. One has been the
Whitehall administrative elite. The senior echelons of the Foreign Office, in particular, have zealously advanced the convergence agenda. For them Europe provided an opening for greater
departmental influence and opportunities for career advancement in the face of shrinking British influence and withdrawal
elsewhere. For many of the Treasury mandarins it provided the
prospect of breaking free of deep-seated constraints that had
long bedevilled the British economy and, through monetary
union, of de-politicising (at least from domestic politics) interest
and exchange-rate policy.

The second group has been the political class for whom
supra-national Europe offered a platform for public prominence
and advancement on the international stage. The third was seen
to be the business community, represented by the Confederation of British Industry. Advantages to business formed the

central plank in the ideology of the continentalists. For thirty years the CBI's enthusiasm for Britain's membership of the EC and the benefits of an expanded 'home' market provided the rationale for the European cause, acting to legitimise the interests of the Foreign Office and administrative elites.

Yet by the time of Maastricht business support had distinctly cooled. Business, even before the traumas of Britain's membership of the ERM, had grown steadily more agnostic and came to endorse a 'minimalist' view of the EC, counter to the pro-Europe ideologues in the Conservative Party and the federalist ambitions of the Foreign Office. For the CBI this was to cause particular problems. It supported the European Movement in the 1975 referendum. It fully endorsed the Single Market legislation of the 1980s. It gave uncritical support for Britain's ERM membership. But as early as the 1970s doubts had set in among the business community over the corporatist nature of the European Commission, and in particular over draft directives which sought to lay down Europe-wide practices in employment and labour relations. Vigorous resistance was mounted by the CBI's rival, the Institute of Directors, against the EC Fifth Directive which would have introduced two-tier management boards with worker representation.

From this point the IoD was to take a distinctly more sceptical view of policy emanating from Brussels than the CBI. It certainly never endorsed the political pretensions of the single currency and the ideology of a federal Europe. The IoD's Director-General Peter Morgan made the point forcefully in a speech to the IoD European centre in October 1993:

> We joined a market. No one, except, perhaps the Foreign Office, understood that we were embarked on a course which could end up with the House of Commons having less power than the state assembly in Ohio.[1]

Throughout the 1970s and 1980s industry was to move from a position of broad support to one of increasing apprehension over many draft directives which were prejudicial to British business interests. The type of Community as promoted by Jacques Delors increasingly came to be seen as socialist, interventionist, bureaucratic, vexatious and costly.

There was particular concern over the uneven way that much of the Single Market legislation was being applied on the continent, and the fact that government subsidies for industries were allowed to continue. Morgan noted:

> The [Single Market] was designed to cure Eurosclerosis – the loss of economic dynamism caused by national barriers to trade. It was designed to improve the competitiveness and productivity of Europe. In reality this is not happening. State aids and subsidies are keeping uncompetitive firms in business, and the whole scene is disrupted by nationalised industries. Since Britain has led the world in privatisation, we are particularly incensed that our telephone companies, our airlines, our banks and insurance companies and our energy companies meet so much regulatory obstruction in the Community, and so much unfair competition from government-supported enterprises.[2]

It was not just the growing anxiety of British firms which had manufacturing plant or operations on the continent and were finding the regulatory climate oppressive, but the failure after thirty years of pro-European rhetoric to create a genuine cross-Channel business community, that led Howard Davies, one of the most pro-European director-generals of the CBI, to admit to an audience of German businessmen in 1993:

> Being a pro-European becomes very difficult, in the face of the drip, drip of criticism and complaint generated by successive directives and regulations. It makes it harder to support the whole process of integration ... just because we [British] are congenitally suspicious of the European Community doesn't mean that it isn't going off the rails.[3]

For the CBI this 'off the rails' candour, together with the quotation from the same speech by Davies at the start of this chapter, marked a distinct retreat. Reconciling this conflict between, on the one hand, representing the interests and concerns of its members over Brussels legislation and, on the other, maintaining good relations with the government, became increasingly difficult. Supportive though it was of the Major government, and under pressure to demonstrate that support during the darkest hours of the Maastricht Bill, it was not about to stand aside and watch all the gains of labour-market reform in the 1980s placed in jeopardy by legislation from Brussels.

Its dilemma was compounded by the fact that it had no wish to help bring down a government that was itself under constant pressure from Brussels to 'prove its European credentials' and see it replaced by one that had pledged itself to implement the Social Chapter provisions in full. Yet the CBI had to make a stand on behalf of British companies if they were not to be left helpless against the tide of damaging Brussels legislation. There thus developed in the CBI a two-tiered address to European convergence: one, in public speeches and statements, which was generally sympathetic to and supportive of the government; and a second, or subtext to these pronouncements. This subtext was to mark the effective abandonment of the CBI's proselytising for Europe and the adoption of a position much closer to that of the IoD. It came to be critical of, and opposed to, much of the EC's legislation in labour and employment affairs, and the CBI's key submissions to the government on Maastricht revealed fundamental differences in attitude and practice between British employers and the thrust of EC legislation.

The extent of the CBI's abandonment of its former position may be gauged by the fact that by the time of the passage of the Maastricht Bill, its Director-General had identified no less than seven areas of business concern over Europe:[4] external trade policy, and in particular German support for French opposition to the GATT agreement; social policy (in particular high levels of social protection and high wage and non-wage costs); the Common Agricultural Policy; state aids to business and the uneven way that Community regulations are enforced; environmental policies biased towards member-states which generate more of their power by non-fossil-fuel means; regional policy (it never worked in spite of the large-scale intra-EC transfers over twenty years) and finally monetary policy.

This list is so comprehensive that it is in retrospect difficult to see how the CBI had come to press for Britain's integration with Europe so uncritically. The CBI's reservations came to be itemised in detail, particularly in the field of social and employment legislation. Central to the EC approach to the Single Market was the development of a single labour market to avoid the enjoyment of unfair trading advantages by member states with less developed systems of protection of employee rights. Without standard employee rights, some member states would, it was felt, enjoy equal access to the EC market but lower employment costs, giving rise to 'social dumping'.

The CBI rejected this approach, arguing that detailed EC-wide regulation of employment practices, labour hiring, working hours and benefits would significantly raise production costs, increase unemployment and worsen the Community's uncompetitiveness in world markets. Its concern focused on the Social Chapter and the Social Action Programme. These were not specific to the Maastricht Treaty but typified the language, style and direction of EC legislation over many years. 'In addition to these questions of principle,' the the CBI declared,

> is the unhappy recognition that over the last ten years and more there have been no EC Commission initiatives in the labour and social affairs field to which Community employers have been able to offer an unequivocal welcome. The reverse has almost invariably been the case. The Commission has brought forward draft proposals the need for which has been undemonstrated, the contribution the measure could make unproven – but the potential cost all too clear.[5]

Its criticisms centred on the Commission's approach to labour regulation and the consequences for competitiveness and employment if applied to Britain. It took as its starting point the EC's falling share of world markets, from more than 25 per cent total OECD exports in 1985 to around 21 per cent in 1993. Moreover this decline was not confined to traditional industries where Europe faced fierce competition from low-cost producers in the emerging market economies but was also evident in high-technology goods. This lack of competitiveness, in the CBI's view, was principally responsible for its growing trade deficits with America and Japan:

> It is grounds for concern that Europe is losing its competitive edge. In terms of shares of world exports of manufactures or in terms of growth in manufacturing productivity, the EC is presently losing its way.[6]

Examples of EC Draft Directives which the CBI felt were inimical to good business in Europe were the Working Time Draft Recommendation (EC-wide regulation of working time arrangements); the Vredeling Draft Directive (on information and consultative procedures); the Fifth Company Law Draft Directive (employee participation in company decision-making) and the Parental Leave Draft Directive (rights for both parents to take leave around and after a birth).

Two were of particular concern to British business. The Working Time Draft Directive set out to contain the working week to 48 hours, provided for rest-breaks during all shifts of over six hours, an eight-hour limit on night shifts, an eleven-hour break in the working day and the prevention 'in principle' of Sunday working. These arrangements would cut across British practice of locally determined, flexible agreements arrived at after consultation with employees. The CBI warned:

> In many different ways the Draft Directive threatens existing good practice; and with it jobs. All costs; no benefits.[7]

Similar objections were raised to the Draft European Works Councils Directive requiring firms above a certain size to comply with time-consuming and often artificial arrangements to handle information and communication across EC boundaries.

Such proposals ran against the grain of the UK labour market which is markedly more decentralised than its continental counterparts and does not lend itself to centralised regulation. The thrust of the Brussels drive for a single labour market is, in the CBI's view,

> inherently interventionist ... the Commission is being drawn inexorably towards Europe-wide regulation of pay. Caveats to the contrary ... carry no conviction: indeed, the Commission has already issued a draft Opinion stating that 'it is appropriate to outline certain basic principles on equitable wages'. Who decides what is equitable? Not the market. Not employers. Not employees.[8]

The CBI also attacked the tendency of the Commission to 'harmonise upwards', enforcing on all countries the most onerous requirements applied in any state regardless of the competitiveness of the enterprise concerned – a sure recipe for pricing people out of jobs. Its most visible – and most wounding – retreat was over Britain's membership of the ERM. Howard Davies admitted:

It was a great defeat for those who thought we might be entering a brave new world of economic policy ... The CBI supported our membership of the ERM until the last minute.[9]

More than 60,000 businesses went under during the recession, many of which could have survived had not rates stayed so high for so long. The experience so scarred the business community that repeated assurances had to be given that no early return to the ERM was planned.

The ERM debacle and its aftermath not only brought an abandonment by the CBI of what many saw as a position of monetary union at any price, but an admonition to those on the continent who sought to carry on as if nothing had changed:

We are told that the Maastricht timetable, unrealistic though it may seem to us, is simply not open for discussion. And that it is axiomatic that a Single Market requires a single currency, a contention which very few people in the United Kingdom would accept. All these arguments look a bit odd to us, to put it no higher than that.[10]

The IoD went further, declaring that it did not expect to see economic and monetary union this century, and advocating instead the introduction of the hard ECU to help companies with cross-border transactions without all the draconian machinery of political union being forced on EC member states by Maastricht.[11]

For the majority of British businessmen the best aspect of Maastricht was not the Treaty but the opt-outs. Whether they will prove watertight remains to be seen. There was concern that the opt-out from the Social Chapter could be nullified by continental firms seeking to impose EC standards on labour employment conditions on Britain through appeal to the European Court.

Similar reservations also apply to the opt-out from Stage Three of economic and monetary union, as Britain would still be required to pursue interest and exchange-rate policies in the common interest of the Community – a requirement that could also be enforced by an appeal to the European Court.

A number of prominent businessmen and City figures were to express opposition to British integration with Europe. Outstanding among these was Sir James Goldsmith, one of

Europe's most successful entrepreneurs. Half French by birth and with a strongly internationalist outlook, the label 'little Englander' was hardly one the supporters of Maastricht could slap on him. His opposition to Maastricht and the EC centralisation was based on two main contentions: first, that by undermining the dynamics of nationhood it threatened social breakdown and conflict, and secondly, that by allowing geographical mobility, it would add to ethnic and political tensions throughout the Community.

A central theme of the campaign to win support for Maastricht was that the City of London would suffer if Britain did not sign up. Ten City grandees, including the Lord Mayor, National Westminster Bank chairman Lord Alexander, the head of Lloyds of London David Rowland, TSB chairman Sir Nicholas Goodison, and S.G. Warburg chairman Sir David Scholey, wrote to *The Times*:

> The overwhelming City view that has emerged is that there are high risks in the UK appearing to disengage from Europe. Businesses from outside the EEC whose European presence is now based in the UK will look elsewhere ...[12]

The letter drew a swift riposte from Professor Alan Walters, formerly chief economic adviser to Mrs Thatcher:

> I suspect it is far more likely that the City will be much more hamstrung and harried by Brussels bureaucrats if the UK is in, rather than out of, the Union ... . Many people, apparently including the Lord Mayor and his co-signatories, believe that any great financial centre must be located within a large hinterland of exchange rate stability for it to prosper. This is quite without foundation.[13]

Anthony Cowgill, Director of the British Management Data Foundation, also attacked the City establishment view:

> It is precisely the open stance and the City's prosperity which are at risk if the UK's institutions are further integrated into Europe. In the light of the debacle of the exchange-rate mechanism, the fact that three of the Lord Mayor's nine co-signatories wrote to [*The Times*] on December 13 1991, stating that 'the economic and monetary union reached at Maastricht is crucial to the economic

well-being of the nation and that it must now be firmly endorsed'
does not inspire confidence in their judgment.[14]

Arguably the most down-to-earth articulation of the British
businessman's view came from Rodney Gilchrist, a senior director of Jardine Matheson:

> I have read with astonishment the frequent assertions that the
> Maastricht Treaty is widely supported by businessmen. Busi-
> nessmen, of course, have the same human frailties as MPs and
> all the rest of us. They are attracted by the prospect of
> knighthoods – even peerages … . They are afraid of being cold-
> shouldered, perhaps losing government contracts or aid to for-
> eign buyers … . The majority of businessmen who have taken the
> trouble to read the Treaty find it a blueprint for an economic and
> political framework diametrically opposed to their own convic-
> tions.
> Businessmen … do not want a protectionist Europe. They
> want to complete and enlarge the single European market, but
> they want also to trade with the wider world, the USA and the
> explosively expanding markets of Asia … . They fear the transfer
> of power to the politicised European Court of Justice … . Busi-
> nessmen have much the same attitude to the Treaty as the
> country at large.[15]

Misgivings were also expressed by those with first-hand
experience of dealings with EC institutions. A striking example
was Dr Ann Robinson, Head of the Policy Unit of the Institute
of Directors. Dr Robinson was for seven years the Welsh Office
representative on the EC Economic and Social Committee based
in Brussels. An ardent pro-European when she took up the
position, her views were to undergo a radical change. This was
her assessment of the EC after seven years 'at the heart':

> The institutional arrangements of the Community are in a mess
> and there is nothing in the Maastricht Treaty which will make
> them work any better. There is widespread inefficiency in the
> way in which EC funds are spent and even evidence of corruption.
> Too much proposed EC legislation is ill-researched, ill-thought-
> out, ill-designed, poorly drafted and hastily rammed through
> with insufficient consultation as to its actual practical effects on
> the ground … . I am not the only person who has started out in
> Brussels full of enthusiasm and who has retired frustrated and
> sceptical about the grand design … . It is all too clear that the

process of creating the EC has been driven by starry-eyed political leaders out of touch with the realities of life ... .

The Maastricht Treaty has provided a focus for popular
discontent but the causes of the EC's present malaise are much
deeper and more complex. No one (not even those who have
read it) can be sure of its implications. It is a colossal blank
cheque ... .

So where is 'Europe' going? I really do not know. We used to
hear an awful lot about the 'European Train'. Apparently it has
a destination but we are not allowed to talk about it. No one
mentions the train now. The train has no clear destination – it's
more like a ghost train going round and round in circles through
a tunnel full of skeletons and spectres. A few of the passengers
are scared out of their wits, others (like me) are jumping out.[16]

But perceptions of support for Maastricht by businessmen
were carefully nurtured during this period, again playing on
fears of the consequences if Britain did not ratify the Treaty. In
March 1993 the CBI circulated a briefing paper to Members of
Parliament claiming that Britain's economic recovery and present and future inward investment from the United States and
Japan depended on ratification of the Treaty.

According to the CBI the report, based on interviews with a
number of companies, all investors from the US and Japan
concluded that 'if the UK fails to ratify the Maastricht Treaty
and it is perceived to be part of a second tier in a two-speed
Europe, this would have a negative effect on half the investors'.
In fact sixteen companies were interviewed and asked what
effect there would be on investment intentions of a two-speed
Europe, Britain not rejoining the ERM and the possibility of
Britain pulling out of the Single Market. To this umbrella
question only 7 per cent said it would have 'a major effect' and
40 per cent 'some effect'.

Another survey by the CBI in the late autumn of 1993 claimed
broad support among businessmen for renewed progress towards EMU. The headline on the CBI's poll findings ('Business
leaders oppose Major on Single Currency') failed to stand up to
scrutiny. As Bill Cash MP pointed out in *The Times*, of the 485
businessmen contacted, 174 replied. Only 12 thought the single
currency would come about by the end of the decade; only nine
said Britain should rejoin the ERM. The rival IoD was quick to
point out out that the CBI survey was also deficient in not

asking respondents what price they were prepared to pay for a return to the ERM.

Arguably a more accurate survey of business opinion at this time came from the European Business Monitor.[17] This survey of 1,500 European business leaders from seven countries found that 68 per cent of British business leaders considered the ERM fatally damaged and believed it would eventually be abandoned. UK business leaders also proved more sceptical than their European counterparts on a single currency. The survey also found considerable scepticism about the benefits of the Single Market (only 12 per cent said there had been any noticeable benefits), while European businessmen as a whole voted Britain as offering the best potential for manufacturing industry.

By early 1994 British business was primarily concerned with domestic economic conditions and the extent to which the recovery would be impaired by the massive programme of tax increases. With the continent showing little sign of recovery from recession, and German, French and Italian interest rates still penally high in real terms, there was little prospect of the European bloc playing a part in, let alone leading, a 'kick start' to the economies of the industrialised world. It was noticeable that no British businessman or City figure joined in the calls made on the continent for the acceleration of the EMU programme after the ERM collapsed in the autumn of 1993.

Through the convergence process British business looked to government as the ultimate guardian of British interests to provide protection from the rain of bureaucratic Euro-directives. But it has been government and the political class that have exposed business to ever greater regulation and control from Brussels. Not only did the CBI fall down on the job of protecting business but it actively promoted the convergence process until it was too late. The fear is now that as the convergence programme rolls on, British business will face more of the same.

Notes

1. Peter Morgan, *The Development of Europe: The IoD Vision*, IoD European Centre & Netherlands Society for Trade and Development, October 1993, section 1.

2. Ibid.

3. Howard Davies, *Britain, Europe and Germany Today*, Industrie-kreis für Auslandsbeziehungen, Dusseldorf, October 1993, p. 2.

4. Ibid., pp. 3-5.

5. *Social Europe After Maastricht: Freedom, Not Licence*, CBI, 1993, p. 11.

6. Ibid., p. 5.

7. Ibid., p. 12.

8. Ibid., p. 13.

9. Howard Davies, op. cit., p. 5.

10. Ibid., p. 6.

11. Morgan, op. cit., section 3.

12. *The Times*, February 18 1993.

13. *The Times*, February 22 1993.

14. *The Times*, February 22 1993.

15. *Sunday Telegraph*, March 1993.

16. Dr Ann Robinson, speech to the Institute of Welsh Affairs/IoD Wales Division, May 20 1993, pp. 7 and 8.

17. *European Business Monitor*, October 1993.

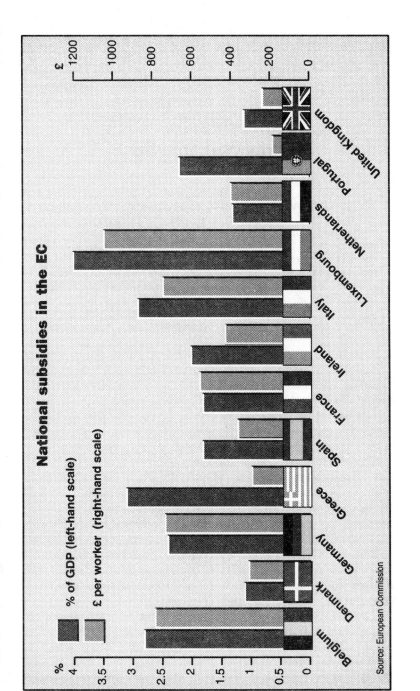

National subsidies in the EC

- % of GDP (left-hand scale)
- £ per worker (right-hand scale)

Belgium, Denmark, Germany, Greece, Spain, France, Ireland, Italy, Luxembourg, Netherlands, Portugal, United Kingdom

£: 0, 200, 400, 600, 800, 1000, 1200

%: 0, 0.5, 1, 1.5, 2, 2.5, 3, 3.5, 4

Source: European Commission

EC Membership: £108 Billion Will Do Nicely

> The government is convinced that our economy will be stronger and our industries and our people more prosperous if we join the European Communities than if we remain outside them ... improvements in efficiency and competitive power should enable the UK to meet the balance-of-payments cost of entry as they gradually build up ... the advantages will far outweigh the costs, provided we seize the opportunities of the far wider home market now open to us.
>
> 1971 White Paper, *The UK and the European Communities*, HMSO

If Britain's application to join the European Community had one potent rationale it was that membership would improve the trade balance and the economy. Industry, in particular, would be able to capitalise on access to a much larger 'home' market which would be governed by the basic rules of free trade. In Britain's post-war history, however, there was never a greater clutch at economic straws and no greater disappointment.

The official justification for Britain's membership of the EC has always been economic, though the ultimate goal is, as it historically always has been, political. The economic advantages claimed for membership have tended to be taken for granted. Yet neither before nor since joining has any formal cost-benefit analysis of EC membership been undertaken by the British government. A gulf has thus arisen between the expansive rhetoric on the benefits of membership and the reality. Failure to submit membership to proper audit has been a cardinal failure of the British Treasury.

The 1971 White Paper on the European Communities gave a cogent summation of the perceived benefits arising from membership of what was claimed to be a free trade bloc but which is deeply protectionist at heart. It was asserted from the start of the debate on membership that linking with the economies of the continent meant a fundamental switch from Britain's historical position as intermediary and arbiter, both between the Commonwealth and the world and the Commonwealth and the EC, largely by virtue of which Britain's wealth and power had been sustained. It was also recognised that EC membership would bring an end to the cheap food drawn from Australia, New Zealand and the Americas in favour of the highly expensive food regime of the EC and, in particular, the Common Agricultural Policy which accounted for almost two-thirds of the total Community budget.[1]

But the central rationale was that the extra cost of food raw materials and products would be more than offset by faster economic growth and the dynamics of volume gain and economies of scale for British industry that an enhanced market of 200 million additional consumers would provide. In this there was an assumption that EC membership would reverse, or at the least bring to an end, the relative economic decline of the UK.

Britain's membership application was supported, not only at the highest levels of the political and diplomatic Establishment but also by the Confederation of British Industry, the chairmen of Britain's largest companies, the Stock Exchange, the clearing banks and leading financial institutions. Since then, a growing body of opinion has come forward to challenge the fundamental assumptions of the economic benefits of membership. Typical of this reappraisal is E.J. Mishan, Emeritus Professor at the London School of Economics:

> The reluctance of successive governments to undertake, or at least to publicise, an economic assessment of Britain's net gains consequent on our membership of the EC is understandable. For notwithstanding the feverish opining of extravagant phrases about the immense economic advantages to be reaped by entry into a Common Market of 'over 200 million customers', the few rough estimates that have been attempted lend no support whatever to these original claims. Quite the contrary, such estimates reveal that ever since we bound ourselves to this economic union, the country has suffered substantial losses, which are certain to grow in the future.[2]

Many claims have been made of the economic gains brought by membership. The benefit most commonly cited is a surge in foreign inward investment to Britain in the 1980s. But this was not a benefit in any way directly conferred from Brussels. Direct foreign investment into the EC rose from less than $28 billion in 1978 to over $197 billion by 1991. But by then it was Britain that was attracting substantially more foreign direct investment than any other EC country, and in 1991 she drew one-third of the EC total. While much of this was by American and Japanese firms using Britain as a springboard for their products into the EC, it also owes much to the more positive attitude towards business taken by the Conservative governments of the 1980s and reforms which were unrelated to EC membership. Prominent among these was the abolition of exchange controls enabling full profits remittance for an overseas company, deregulation, capital allowances and reductions in Corporation Tax to the lowest in Europe.

Similarly the reforms of the 1980s, most notably in the field of labour relations, brought a competitive spur to UK industry. The decade was to see marked improvements not only in price competitiveness, but in quality, design, technology and delivery, Britain's industrial performance improved markedly.

Of the growth of UK exports within the EC since entry the figures appear impressive. Between 1970 and 1990 they rose from £2.3 billion, or 20 per cent of total exports, to more than £40 billion or just over 50 per cent. However, during this period the Community itself was substantially enlarged, with the accession, among others, of Ireland, Denmark, Spain, Portugal and Greece, and it would have been startling indeed had Britain's exports to a rapidly expanding EC not increased.

After twenty years of membership every single one of the benefits advanced in favour of membership of the EC – a faster rate of economic growth, higher living-standards, a break-out from chronic balance-of-payments deficits and greater influence in the world – have proved unfounded or, at best, under that inestimably useful classification of Scottish law: Not Proven.

On any examination the cost of membership has been ferocious for Britain. It has severely worsened the country's balance of payments. Through a brief but turbulent membership of the ERM, interest rates were determined by German more than by domestic monetary conditions and forced thousands of companies into bankruptcy. It has added to unemployment and has increasingly tied Britain into a high-cost, uncompetitive economic bloc whose share of world trade is falling. It has forced Britain down a road towards economic and monetary union which would permanently strip its institutions of sovereignty over such key levers of economic control as monetary policy and interest rates. And it has threatened Britain's historical role as a global trading nation in favour of integration with one of the world's most notoriously inefficient, costly and protectionist farming lobbies, the CAP. For a world view we have substituted a blinkered regional one. And our standing in the world, far from being enhanced by membership, is being subsumed in a protectionist Fortress Europe mentality and structure. The total direct financial cost to Britain of EC membership is now £108 billion. This comprises a cumulative visible balance of payments deficit with the EC since 1973 of £87 billion (see table 8.1 on p. 110) and net financial contributions to the Community budget of £21 billion.

The lofty rhetoric of the 1971 White Paper, of advantages far outstripping costs was to fall far short of reality. As economists Brian Burkitt, Mark Baimbridge and Stephen Reed concluded:

> Experience proved these sentiments to be nothing more than unrealistic assertions built upon faith rather than evidence or reason. These forecasted dynamic gains are nowhere to be seen. The relative decline of British manufacturing not only continued but accelerated. The UK's economic growth has been constrained since its accession to the EC by persistent problems on its international trading account ... .
> ... The EC, particularly Germany, accounts for the UK's trading difficulties, since the UK normally enjoys a surplus with the rest of the world. Therefore the economic promise offered by EC membership proved to be a mirage.[3]

Balance-of-payments damage

Even during the pre-entry negotiations it was clear that the full impact would imply 'a deterioration in the current account and possibly a deterioration in the long-term capital account of the balance of payments'.[4] To tackle this, Britain would have to devalue or cut public spending to achieve a demand deflation sufficient to offset the adverse balance-of-payments impact of entry. The hope had been that, in some way, higher growth would bring dynamic gains, on the proviso that productivity in the UK grew faster than the EC average. However, the gains were difficult to quantify. There was no perceptible gain during the first seven years of entry. Between 1972 and 1979 Gross National Product per head fell from 85 per cent to 78 per cent of the EC average: 'Any belief in the benefits of entry', concluded economists A.R. Prest and D.J. Coppock, 'remains a matter of faith.'[5]

One evident result was an acceleration of a swing of UK trade from the Commonwealth to the economies of Western Europe. Between 1970 and 1973 UK exports to the EC grew at a compound annual rate of 19 per cent, while imports rose by 27 per cent. There was an overall visible trade deficit with the EC over these years of £726 million. Between 1973 and 1979 the overall deficit on visible trade with the EC grew to £14.7 billion.

Most assessments of the initial impact of entry on the balance of payments have focused on the costs associated with the Common Agricultural Policy. Under the CAP Britain had to import all foodstuffs at common EC prices and to impose import levies on goods from non-EC sources. At the time Britain entered, EC prices were between 18 per cent and 26 per cent higher than those in the world market, and the adverse balance of payments impact was reckoned at between £175 million and £250 million. However, this impact was mitigated by a rise in world food prices in the immediate years after Britain's entry.

But there was a growing opportunity cost of loss of Commonwealth and world markets. Most of this trade involved the import of raw materials and foodstuffs in exchange for exports of industrial manufactured goods and equipment. By joining the EC Britain gave up this source of raw materials and potential for value added in favour of the exchange of manufactured goods with the EC. This at once both aggravated the balance of payments and increased domestic unemployment as consumer demand was met by manufactured imports. Between 1970 and 1979 there was a growing deterioration in Britain's balance of trade in manufactures. This went from a surplus of £385 million to a deficit of £3.4 billion. By 1990 there was a deficit with the EC in manufactures of £8.5 billion. By the end of the 1980s Germany had replaced the United States as Britain's leading trading partner. But this change, bringing with it a surge in German exports to Britain further contributed to the worsening of Britain's trade deficit. Thus, although there was an increase in trade, imports continued to grow more quickly than exports.

Between 1981 and 1992 the UK ran an overall deficit of £83 billion with the EC. The swing towards EC trade, and with it the enhanced propensity to import Continental European finished manufactures, aggravated an already weak British balance-of-payments position and increased pressure for sterling depreciation throughout the 1970s. More recently continental recession brought a weakening in the UK exports to the EC so that by the final quarter of 1993 exports to non-EC countries had closed the gap.

The economists Burkitt, Baimbridge and Reed[6] examined the effects on a number of UK industries. In 1970 import penetration of the UK home market for cars stood at 5 per cent. By 1990 it had shot to 51 per cent. UK output of cars fell from 1.9 million in 1972 to 1.29 million in 1989. This reduction had knock-on effects throughout the supply and servicing industries. In 1973 each Ford, Vauxhall or Peugeot Talbot car had an average UK component content of 91 per cent. By 1984 it was down to 34 per cent. In 1990 the UK motor industry's trade deficit was a record £6.5 billion, mostly created by multinationals importing from the EC. While there are many complex factors at work to account for this deterioration, not least our own failure to exploit trading opportunities, it was not at all the result that the government and the corporate sector had gone out of their way to encourage the British people to expect. Britain's iron and steel industry saw import penetration jump from 11 per cent in 1975 to 34.5 per cent in 1990, its relative decline ascribed to the structure of EC production quotas and system of minimum prices which prevented Britain increasing its share of the EC market – the exact opposite of free trade.

Import penetration and a worsening trade balance with the Community has been experienced in goods where Britain has a competitive edge and has fared well in non-EC world markets such as telecommunications equipment, aircraft manufacture, chemicals and machine tools. Britain's trade surplus with the rest of the world in telecom equipment, for example, grew from £61 million in 1970 to £719 million in 1989, while trade with the EC went from a surplus of £3 million to a deficit of £851 million over the same period (see table 8.3 on p. 112).

The Common Agricultural Policy

The Common Agricultural Policy, the centrepiece of Fortress Europe, came into being in 1964 after years of agonising negotiation. It had the conflicting objectives of 'ensuring a fair standard of living for the agricultural community'; 'stable markets'; 'continuity of supplies'; and 'to ensure supplies to consumers at reasonable prices'.

It was essentially the outcome of a bargain struck between France and West Germany under which the industrial market of the original Six would be open to the Germans while French farmers were protected by a common agricultural market sealed off from external competition. The notion that Britain could achieve major reform once in the Community always looked doubtful on this perspective.

Immediately before Britain's application to join, EC farm prices were higher than world prices by more than 30 per cent for poultry, 75 per cent for beef, 85 per cent for wheat, 100 per cent for oilseeds, nearly 300 per cent for butter and 340 per cent for white sugar. These prices enshrined one of the most costly and inefficient systems of agricultural protectionism in the world. Throughout the 1980s the Community persisted in maintaining subsidies to food producers well above the American level – the root cause of trade friction between the two continents.

The CAP accounts for two-thirds of the Community budget and has been a major source of contention. In 1990 it cost more than £19 billion to administer. Even before 1970 surpluses of cereals, dairy products, sugar and wine began to emerge as production, underpinned by guaranteed prices, outstripped demand.

Various attempts have been made to reduce the grotesque stockpiles created by the CAP and to reform the system. They have ended in failure. The economist Richard Howarth in his assessment of the CAP noted:

Across Europe in May 1991 refrigerated stores, including ships with chilled holds moored off Cork in Ireland and silos were once again overflowing with 800,000 tonnes of dairy products, 800,000 tonnes of beef and 19 million tonnes of grain. By the end of September intervention stocks of beef (865,000 tonnes) were at a record level.[7]

Estimates by the National Consumer Council suggested that by 1988, as a result of the CAP, the weekly spending on food of a British family of four was £13.50 a week higher. By 1990 the burden was reckoned at £16. Throughout the 1980s food prices within the EC were on average 70 per cent higher than those in the world market. A 1993 OECD estimate calculates that an average UK family of four is paying about £1,040 a year – or £20 a week more – on food as a result of the CAP and its end purpose of protecting inefficient farmers in Germany and France.

By 1993 the estimated gross bill was more than £88 billion, divided among the nine million employed by the CAP and paid for by the remaining 320 million.

Britain and the EC Budget

Since joining the Community in 1973 Britain has been a net contributor in virtually every single year. Because Britain is more dependent on imports from non-EC countries it pays a disproportionate share of levies and duties.

In 1984, amid charges of being a 'bad' European, Prime Minister Margaret Thatcher tenaciously fought for a reduction in Britain's contribution. Not only was the gross contribution soaring but the net amount after refunds and public sector receipts multiplied from £100 million in 1973 to almost £1 billion by 1979. The early years of the 1980s saw a decrease. But by 1986 Britain's net contribution almost trebled in one year to £1.8 billion. The means by which Britain's net contribution was to be reduced was the European Regional Development Fund. Britain was initially awarded a quota of 28 per cent. But other EC countries came to oppose increases in the ERDF and the accession of Greece, Portugal and Spain markedly increased the competition for ERDF cash, so that Britain's quota was reduced to 16.9 per cent.

For 1993-94 the Treasury has estimated Britain's net payment at £2.45 billion. This is forecast, according to the November 1993 Budget Red Book, to fall to £1.3 billion in 1994-95 before rising to £2.9 billion for each of the years 1995-96 and 1996-97.[8]

Although Continental European economies were experiencing worsening recession in the first half of 1993, the Community budget is set to expand at an accelerating rate. Expenditure is forecast to grow for the five years starting in 1993 to cover the costs of the constitutional changes in the Maastricht Treaty. The expansion will be from £36 billion in 1987 to £47 billion in 1992 and to £62 billion in 1997. Barring an overhaul in the EC and the budget, it is doubtful if Britain will see extra benefit, while its contributions will continue to rise.

Costs of the ERM

Arguably the most penal aspect of growing European integration was Britain's membership of the Exchange Rate Mechanism. The issue is dealt with more fully elsewhere, but suffice to say here that whatever gains were enjoyed by savings on transaction costs – just 0.4 per cent of GDP according to the EC Commission's own calculations – these were lost in the hurricane of higher borrowing costs, falling business orders and soaring bankruptcies.

The recession in Britain was more severe than in any other English-speaking country. Unemployment rose to almost three million with a consequent increase in welfare spending and a worsening of Britain's budget deficit, which climbed to £37 billion in the year to April 1993 and on to £48 billion in 1993-94.

The cost to the reserves of defending sterling in the final weeks of ERM membership is estimated at around £2 billion. Other estimates put the cost to the reserves at between £4 billion and £6 billion.[9] The corporate sector benefited immediately from the policy relaxation which followed. By January 1993, when interest rates were cut to 6 per cent, industry was enjoying a cumulative reduction of £4 billion in interest costs as a result of interest-rate reductions after the exit from the ERM when they had been held at 10 per cent, a level which gave real interest rates of 6 per cent.

Loss of competitiveness

By the early 1990s the business sector was expressing increasing unease about high labour costs in the EC and the resulting loss of competitiveness and world market share. The concerns are threefold: first, that the EC has had a declining share of world markets for more than ten years; second, it has become a region of slow productivity growth; and third, EC non-wage labour costs are particularly high and push total labour costs up to non-competitive levels. These concerns became increasingly evident as recession deepened throughout the Continent in 1993. While the CBI welcomed Britain's negotiation of the opt-out clause on the Social Chapter there was widespread unease that the provisions of the Social Chapter would come to be introduced 'through the back Delors'.

The slide in the EC's share of world trade has been pronounced. While trade between EC countries grew 40 per cent between 1985 and 1991, the growth of EC exports to other countries has, in the CBI's words, 'been dismal'. Since 1985 EC export volumes have actually fallen by 3 per cent. Exports of high-technology goods to countries outside the EC has been particularly weak, growing by just 4 per cent since 1985.

The Community now runs substantial trade deficits with the United States and Japan. In 1985 it had a surplus in US trade of 0.5 per cent of its GDP. By 1990 this had become a deficit, and is now the equivalent of 2 per cent of GDP. A major contributor has been the trend in EC manufacturing productivity. While this increased by around 3 per cent a year throughout the 1980s, the US and Japan were achieving 4 per cent and 5 per cent a year growth respectively.

Summary

A marked worsening of the balance of payments, heavy and increasing gross and net payments to the EC budget, and a brief, fatal experiment with semi-fixed exchange rates have cost Britain dear. Not only has there been no sign of the enhanced efficiency benefits that were predicted 'in the long term', but the 1992 Single Market has fallen short of expectations. Far from the progress towards economic and monetary union creating stability and prosperity, the ERM has been punctuated by periods of volatility and, as we examine later, helped push Continental Europe deeper into recession.

There has not been the break-out from balance-of-payments crises that had been looked for. Nor is there much sign that membership of the EC will do anything other than intensify Britain's economic predicament.

Membership has also proved a disappointment to many companies which hoped it would be easier to expand on the Continent through acquisition. Legal, regulatory and institutional barriers to take-over are formidable. Many German and French companies are enmeshed in sizeable and complex cross share-holdings with banks and financial institutions, while inability to break through into Continental distribution channels has been a frequent difficulty, particularly for the financial services sector.

A notable casualty has been the fishing industry, where Britain's right to control fishing in its waters has been ceded to Brussels with a resulting decline in the size of the UK industry. An Act of Parliament designed to prevent the poaching of the quotas of British fishermen by Continentals has been declared illegal by the Luxembourg Court. The British fishing fleet is only able to engage in two days' legal fishing per week, in the supposed interests of conservation of fishing stocks.

But the most widely perceived feature of membership has been a deluge of bureaucratic controls and regulations affecting all sectors of the economy, from foodstuffs to office furniture and water to supermarket labelling. Britain has groaned under a growing weight of petty Euro-regulation and Euro-directives and costly interference. Euro-regulations have hit thousands of enterprises throughout the economy, from slaughterhouses to retailing. The water industry has been concerned at the arbitrary imposition of new standards and controls that would substantially increase the costs to consumers. In 1993 a summary appeared of EC directives on working conditions in offices, running to 45 pages, ranging from the use of electricity to compulsory display of notices. New office 'Euro-chairs' have been prescribed, with exact measurements for seating and posture. Adam Smith-style free trade contributing to the wealth of nations it was not. The cost has been considerable and the burden on enterprise vexatious.

As great as all these, however, has been the opportunity cost of EC membership. It has distracted Britain from the pressing truth that her economic problems are for herself to solve. The expectation that membership would help break Britain free of balance-of-payments crises and relative decline has proved false. But greater than the loss of faith has been the loss of British spirit and morale.

Notes

1. Sidney Pollard, *The Development of the British Economy*, 3rd ed., *1914-1980*, 1983, pp. 368-71.

2. E.J. Mishan, *Salisbury Review*, March 1993.

3. Burkitt, Baimbridge and Reed, *From Rome to Maastricht: A Reappraisal of Britain's Membership of the European Community*, Campaign for an Independent Britain, 1992, p. 3.

4. Prest and Coppock, *The UK Economy. A Manual of Applied Economics*, 1980, pp. 156-7.

5. Ibid., p. 163.

6. Burkitt, Baimbridge and Reed, op. cit., pp. 10 f.

7. Richard Howarth, 'The Common Agricultural Policy', in *The Cost of Europe*, ed. Patrick Minford, 1992, p. 59.

8. HM Financial Statement and Budget Report, 1994-95, November 1993, H.M. Treasury.

9. See *Central Banking* magazine, vol. III, no. 2, Autumn 1992, p. 14.

TABLE 8.1
BRITAIN'S TRADE BALANCE WITH THE EC

year	exports (£m)	imports (£m)	EC trade balance (£m)
1970	2,348	2,304	44
1971	2,512	2,697	−185
1972	2,836	3,421	−585
1973	3,943	5,124	−1,181
1974	5,581	7,608	−2,027
1975	6,273	8,676	−2,403
1976	9,025	11,129	−2,104
1977	12,414	14,223	−1,809
1978	14,059	16,545	−2,486
1979	18,084	20,793	−2,709
1980	21,467	20,710	757
1981	21,938	21,853	85
1982	24,267	25,442	−1,175
1983	27,957	30,417	−2,460
1984	32,962	36,060	−3,098
1985	37,902	39,958	−2,056
1986	34,751	43,162	−8,411
1987	39,021	48,031	−9,010
1988	40,904	54,455	−13,551
1989	47,296	62,266	−14,970
1990	54,377	64,231	−9,854
1991	58,584	59,219	−535
1992	60,365	64,022	−3,657
1993	63,500	67,411	−3,911
1970-91			−87,291

TABLE 8.2
UK NET CONTRIBUTIONS TO THE EC BUDGET

year	net contribution (£m)
1973	102
1974	29
1975	−56
1976	167
1977	369
1978	822
1979	947
1980	706
1981	397
1982	606
1983	647
1984	656
1985	1,808
1986	572
1987	1,721
1988	1,362
1989	2,315
1990	2,475
1991	545
1992	2,599
1993	2,450*
Total	21,239

* Treasury Red Book estimate, November 1993

TABLE 8.3

EC: LOSING GROUND IN PRODUCTIVITY

percentage annual change in value added per person unemployed			
	1980-85	1985-90	1980-90
West Germany	2.6	2.0	2.3
Italy	1.8	3.3	2.5
Spain	4.7	0.3	2.5
France	2.1	3.2	2.6
UK	5.4	4.0	4.7
EEC average	3.5	2.4	2.9
United States	4.4	3.6	4.0
Japan	6.0	3.9	4.9

Source: OECD and CBI estimates.

TABLE 8.4

EC: HIGH EMPLOYMENT COSTS

Hourly compensation in manufacturing $ per hour worked			
	pay for time worked	holiday pay etc.	social insurance	total
Germany	12.27	4.50	4.76	21.53
Italy	8.27	2.90	5.24	16.41
France	8.32	2.56	4.35	15.23
US	10.83	0.96	4.90	14.77
Japan	7.36	2.11	3.17	12.64
UK	9.15	1.48	1.80	12.43
Asian NIEs[*]	3.40		0.35	3.75

[*] Hong Kong, Korea, Singapore, Taiwan.

Source: US Bureau of Labor Statistics.

Europe: Convergence on the Dole

From the late 1980s the British Cabinet, the City, the Confederation of British Industry, the Bank of England, the Chancellor and the Treasury had united on a policy of economic and monetary integration with Europe. Its chosen instrument was the Exchange Rate Mechanism. Seldom had there been an Establishment consensus more powerful, and seldom was such a consensus to be so humiliated.

Not only did it come to inflict upon Britain the worst recession since the war, but to the end it maintained that the alternative to it would be even deeper recession, higher interest rates, higher unemployment, a flight of capital and higher inflation. But it was due to Britain's expulsion from the ERM and with it the collapse of the consensus that Britain was the first EC country to come out of recession. It entered 1994 with falling unemployment, interest rates more than halved since September 1992, a stock market boom and inflation not only the lowest in Europe but the lowest seen in Britain for 26 years. Economic growth in Britain exceeded that of all the main European economies in 1993 and looked set to repeat the performance in 1994.

This collapse of Establishment consensus exposed not only the folly of politically-set timetables for monetary union, but also critical flaws at the heart of the convergence agenda. It was because of that agenda that 1993, the first year of the much-vaunted European Single Market, proved to be the worst for Europe's economies since the war, with unemployment climbing to more than 18 million.

In the late 1980s the EC member states extolled the Single Market as the key to sustained growth. Financial deregulation and integration, improved access to markets, and enhanced business confidence would result in greater investment, job creation and prosperity. Similar claims surrounded the ERM, the instrument by which currencies, monetary policy and interest rates across the continent were to be brought into alignment. By linking their currencies to the anti-inflation anchor of the Deutschemark, the economies of Europe would benefit from enhanced prospects for low inflation, interest-rate convergence and exchange-rate stability.

But by 1993 Europe was deep in recession. Unemployment was at the highest level since the 1930s, with the OECD forecasting that it would rise to 12 per cent – a total of 22 million out of work. In Germany the trend of unemployment is relentlessly up, the totals climbing to 10 per cent in the west and 17 per cent in the east. The economy has suffered its first fall in Gross Domestic Product since 1975. Output tumbled more than 10 per cent year-on-year and manufacturing orders by 11 per cent. Companies such as Daimler-Benz, Mercedes, Krupp and BASF have experienced unprecedented falls in business while corporate failures, which hit a post-war record of 15,000 in 1993, are expected to rise to 19,000 in 1994. The need for a re-financing of Metallgesellschaft, one of Germany's largest companies, was dramatic evidence of Germany's crisis.

Conventional explanations put the blame on the global downturn while some, such as Deutsche Bank, blamed the cost of German reunification.[1] But reunification was not the primary cause of the problems that were to beset Germany and Europe.

Any malaise in Germany casts a shadow across the continent. Its economy accounts for a quarter of Europe's Gross Domestic Product, 40 per cent of its manufacturing output and 35 per cent of its exports. More than 20 per cent of all French exports go to Germany. For Italy the figure is 21 per cent, for the Netherlands 29 per cent. The most potent link is monetary. Through the ERM Germany's central bank set interest rates across the whole of Europe. And in the early 1990s German interest rates, kept high to bear down on fiscal expansion resulting from reunification, came to inflict severe damage on all the EC economies. France suffered its worst slowdown since the Second World War with high real interest rates and severe unemployment. Italy, seized by corruption scandals which brought near-paralysis to its government, was caught in the grip of spiralling debt which ballooned to 110 per cent of GDP, exceeding that under Mussolini. In Spain industrial output slumped and unemployment climbed to over 16 per cent. In the Netherlands gross public debt in 1993 climbed to almost 80 per cent of GDP.

But the continental economies, particularly Germany, were starting to underperform well before reunification, suffered more severely than the Anglo-Saxon economies and continued to suffer after the Anglo-Saxon economies were starting to recover. Was recession on the continent primarily cyclical at all, or the product of a deeper, structural disorder? The longer Europe's economic downturn has persisted the more evident it became that the continent was in the grip of a recession that was not the product of global economic downturn but the complex interaction of three factors peculiar to the EC.

The first was a growing problem of competitiveness which had been mounting for two decades and which was to be given a tongue-twisting but memorable name: *Eurosclerosis*. This was to be aggravated within Germany by high taxes and social security contributions following reunification. The second was the conflict between loose fiscal and tight monetary policy in Germany. And the third was the transmission of this disinflationary mismatch to other EC members' economies through the device of the ERM.

Thus the drive to economic and monetary union, far from being a passive casualty of the recession, was the means by which Europe's crisis of competitiveness and labour-market rigidity was heightened and accelerated. Indeed it has been the convergence agenda itself, and the push for integration culminating in the Maastricht Treaty that transmitted and deepened recession throughout the ERM currency bloc.

But long before reunification there was growing evidence that the German economic miracle was fading and that its economy was heading for trouble. The peak decade for West Germany was 1950-1960 when its economy achieved growth averaging 8.2 per cent a year. Over the same period the French economy grew by an average 4.6 per cent a year and that of Britain by 2.8 per cent. But from then on, the German economy began to lose its outstanding dynamism. According to Merrill Lynch economist Holger Schmieding,[2] the trend rate of growth declined continuously into the early 1980s. From 1960 to the first oil price shock of 1973, West Germany's growth rate almost halved while all other countries except Italy managed to improve their growth performance relative to the 1950s. From the late 1950s to the late 1980s, West Germany was out-performed by France. In the decade 1980 to 1990, average annual growth in Germany at 1.9 per cent was out-paced by France (2.1 per cent), Italy (2.3 per cent), the United Kingdom (2.7 per cent), the United States (3 per cent) and Japan (4.2 per cent). Ironically, the critical argument advanced by the Establishment and the continentalists for greater UK integration with the EC was the perceived high growth-rate of West Germany – an outdated perception, it was to prove.

On the continent the driving force behind European monetary union was political. When French President Valéry Giscard d'Estaing and German Chancellor Helmut Schmidt reached agreement in the late 1970s to launch the European Monetary System, their intention was primarily to reinforce European institutions. Political idealism took precedence over economic fundamentals.

German reunification was to have a galvanising effect on the push for convergence. With the prospect of a reunified Germany, France in particular was anxious to ensure that the new greater Germany was 'tied in, tied up and tied down'. The greatest exponent of the federal agenda was European Commission president, Jacques Delors, former French finance minister under Mitterrand and a fervent believer in planning, interventionism and a Europe-wide code of welfare and employment legislation. Delors was the leading exponent of the school that believed economic success could be legislated into existence by social-welfare and social-chapter provisions. Above all he was zealous in the promotion of European institutions and the strengthening of their power and functions as a means of achieving convergence throughout the EC.

The climax of this phase of integration enthusiasm was the Maastricht Treaty with targets set for economic and monetary union. By 1997 Europe's leading economies were to have brought down their budget deficits to within 3 per cent of GDP; government debt to within 60 per cent of GDP and inflation down to within 1.5 per cent of the best in Europe. At the time of Maastricht, the lowest inflation rate was Germany's, at 2.7 per cent.

Convergence did not just hold out the conventional political rewards that growth and falling unemployment historically offered. It provided a means of asserting Europe in the intensifying politics of global regionalism. It also presented a greater political prize: an opportunity to rise above the confines of narrow domestic agendas to prominence on a supra-national plane.

The political classes of Denmark, Spain, Italy and the Benelux countries, barely known beyond their borders, would gain in stature by becoming part of a Euro-elite that would have global recognition, conferring on its membership status and power greater than the local domestic stage could provide. It is this dimension, arguably more than any other, that explains the insistent, self-renewing pressure for pan-European supranationalism.

But the political approach was blind to the way that growing social-security, employment and labour-relations legislation and the full panoply of welfare politics had impaired the ability of European economies to respond to changes in world markets and in particular the competitive challenge from the emerging economies of the Far East and, nearer home, the newly liberated economies of Central and Eastern Europe with their low cost base.

Europe's crisis, far from originating with German reunification and world recession, had deeper roots. Unemployment had been rising long before the late 1980s. In each economic cycle since the second half of the 1960s the underlying level of unemployment in the continent had risen, from 2.5 per cent in the late 1960s to 4 per cent in the 1970s and to nearly 10 per cent in the 1980s. This was not only far steeper than the rises experienced in the United States and Japan, but the level in absolute terms was significantly higher.

Well before reunification it was evident that not enough jobs were being created in Europe to match the increase in the labour force. By 1991 long-term unemployment in the EC stood at 45 per cent of the total unemployed, compared with 18 per cent in Japan and only 6 per cent in the United States.[3]

Over-regulation of Europe's labour markets has been a major factor. The EC's labour costs rose by 4 per cent a year during the 1980s compared with 0-1 per cent in Japan and the United States. EC wage and non-wage costs are also higher by some 20 per cent than in Japan and the US. Since 1985 productivity in the EC has grown by less than 3 per cent a year, against 4 per cent in the United States and almost 5 per cent in Japan.

Thus it was not the 'crisis of re-unification' but a long-term corrosion of its competitive edge brought about by social and labour legislation that resulted in systemic high and growing unemployment throughout the EC in the 1990s and an intensifying labour shake-out in German manufacturing industry. Even the *Economist*, which has vigorously championed the cause of European integration, constantly berating Britain for her un-European ways, felt an ominous subsidence underfoot. In a world where capital can move freely, investment and technology will go wherever labour is skilled, and cheap and West German rates, it pointed out, were the highest in the world.

When countries lose their competitive edge manufacturing is hardest hit because it is the part of the economy most vulnerable to international competition. This is especially damaging to Europe because Germany has so much of its workforce in manufacturing – more than any other industrialised country. Plans by BMW and Mercedes to build new car plants in South Carolina are only two of the warning bells that have sounded across Europe. At the proposed Mercedes plant the labour cost per car will be a third of what it is in Germany.

Volkswagen was to prove a classic case study. In 1988, when the Bonn government sold off its last 16 per cent holding in the car giant it was widely hailed as a move that would lead to action being taken at last to reduce costs. At the time VW's profit margin was one-third that of its main competitors. But little was done. A 20 per cent holding remained in the hands of the Lower Saxony government, currently an SDP/Green Party co-alition. This, together with worker representatives on the board, still presides over the company's affairs. According to the *Financial Times*, 'As a result, Volkswagen has continued to be run more in the style of a social security office than a commercial concern. Even today its in-house pay agreement was the most generous in the German car industry.'[4] The long delay in taking remedial action was to prove penal. In 1993 the company shed 20,000 jobs across its six German plants as part of a management plan to knock out costs of DM 8.7 billion.

The Maastricht Treaty committed the EC to seeking an increasing level of social protection. But, as a UK Treasury and Department of Employment study noted,[5] public social security and health-care expenditure as a proportion of GDP is already nearly twice as high as in Japan and 60 per cent more than in the United States. Moreover spending on social security and health care in the EC has grown faster than GDP. Europe's loss of competitiveness is the reason why it has been declining both absolutely and in relation to its global competitors. Since 1985 exports from the EC have fallen in volume terms by 3 per cent. In 1985 the EC ran a trade surplus with the United States equivalent to 0.5 per cent of its GDP. By 1990, that is, before the 'trauma of reunification' had begun to be felt, this had become a deficit.

A similar deterioration is evident in the trade balance with Japan. As a result, the EC's share of OECD exports has fallen from just over 25 per cent to around 21 per cent, and with the world as a whole it runs a trade deficit of almost 2 per cent of its GDP. Investment in research and development is lower in Europe than in Japan or America. Since 1987 Europe has been running a trade deficit in high-technology goods. In other words, technology is not making up for Europe's high labour costs.

European convergence politics has aggravated this lack of competitiveness and catalysed a labour shake-out across the continent. The main mechanism of accelerated convergence was to be the ERM. Member countries would fix their currencies to the anchor currency of the Deutschemark. By limiting the movement of their currencies to within a narrow band either side of the Deutschemark they could hitch themselves to this star of monetary virtue. Domestic interest-rate policy would be dictated by the requirement to keep their currencies within this band. In this way vice was punished and virtue rewarded.

In October 1990, under the Chancellorship of John Major, Britain formally joined the ERM, notwithstanding that informal DM-tracking had done nothing to check a monetary and inflationary expansion. Yet across the economic and political Establishment the ERM was hailed as a vital and welcome cutting-edge external discipline.

Meanwhile in Germany reunification unfolded with a speed which belied the enormous differences between the two economies and the extent and expense of the restructuring involved. Wages in East Germany were typically around 36 per cent of West German levels at the time of reunification. By 1991 they were up to 46 per cent. Labour unions were pressing for – and achieving – agreements giving near to full convergence of wage

levels within three to five years. As serious for the economy was
the fact that pay parity deals were being struck without commensurate improvements in productivity. Each East German
worker was reckoned to be producing only 30 per cent of his
counterpart in the west. But average wage levels in eastern
Germany have risen by 80 per cent since reunification. Soon the
implosion of the eastern economy began to be felt. The overall
impact of reunification on the German government finances has
thus been colossal. In 1990 Germany had a total public sector
deficit of DM 88 billion, equivalent to 3.6 per cent of GDP. By
1992 it had shot to DM 184 billion or more than 6 per cent of
GDP. As a raft of work and welfare benefits, the fruit of an
earlier era of prosperity in West Germany, were applied to the
East, the Bundesbank soon had to contend with a surge in
inflation. By late 1991 Germany's broad money supply was
rising above target, finally reaching 11 per cent in 1992. Interest
rates were thus raised to dampen credit demand and the borrowing surge fuelled by reunification.

Prospects for deep and speedy German interest rate cuts –
for which the whole of Europe was now desperate – had van-
ished as the German budget deficit climbed. Throughout 1992
the Bundesbank came under increasing pressure from other
ERM countries to lower rates. In the Bundesbank's view such
pressure was misplaced. If it gave in, not just German monetary
stability was at risk but Europe would no longer have an anchor
currency worth the name. By making the Deutschemark the
anchor, the ERM had effectively transformed the German central bank into a European institution accountable to other
European governments. But the Bundesbank was the creation of
the German government, with statutory obligations to control
inflation within Germany. It may well be the most powerful
institution in Europe. But it can never be a European institution.

In Britain, post-Conservative re-election euphoria about recovery quickly evaporated amid evidence of deepening recession
and a billowing budget deficit. The irony of Britain's position
was that it had swapped German monetary targeting for its
own. Europe, it seemed, was being bled by the Bundesbank and
the atavistic pay demands of German steelworkers and former
Communist civil servants – and when labour costs the world
over were falling.

In the early weeks of September overnight money-market

rates in Europe shot to penal levels to preserve ERM parities. The German central bank, under the terms of the ERM, spent some DM 24 billion trying to rescue the Lira from collapse but the Italians were forced out, followed soon after by the British. Most estimates put the cost to Britain of the defence of the ERM parity at around £2 billion, though some authoritative sources put it as high as £6 billion.[6]

Britain's expulsion from the ERM was a devastating blow to the credibility of the Prime Minister and in particular of his Chancellor Norman Lamont, who was replaced seven months later. But very soon recovery began to be seen. A lingering rump of ERM apologists argued that the recovery was already underway before September. In fact, while second quarter GDP showed an improvement on the first three months of 1992, the figure was 0.8 per cent down on the level a year earlier and third quarter GDP was 0.2 per cent lower. It was not until the fourth quarter that GDP ceased to show a decline on the corresponding period a year before. Other measures also date recovery from the fourth quarter of 1992. The first fall in unemployment was recorded in February 1993, four months after Britain's expulsion from the ERM. Retail sales, which picked up temporarily on the Conservative election victory in May 1992, fell back during the summer months, and it was not until January 1993, following the reductions in interest rates, that retail sales showed a steady and sustained improvement. October 1992 also marked the worst point for house prices. From that month the fall in prices, as measured by the Halifax House Price Index, began to moderate.

Meanwhile the government, badly bruised by the events of September, complained of 'fault lines' in the ERM, a dissembling euphemism given the scale of the deflationary havoc and the extent to which the ERM had destabilised economies and governments throughout Europe. Everyone was desperate not to wreck the ratification of the Maastricht Treaty and its timetable for convergence. This was the constant reaffirmation and refrain. The political dictates of Maastricht overrode all other considerations and shut the minds of Europe's leadership to the underlying structural problems in their economies.

A lofty insouciance was maintained to the end. A report on the ERM, drafted by a committee of European central bank governors and published in the early summer of 1993, concluded that 'current institutional and technical arrangements in the EMS remain on the whole appropriate', a wholly vacuous and absurd assessment that flew in the face of the evidence. Not only is there now no realistic prospect of the ERM countries complying with the Maastricht timetable but the action required to bring these deficit levels down points to substantial reductions in government spending and/or tax increases.

Soon thé ERM was engulfed in another crisis. France, denied scope for further interest-rate cuts, grew desperate as the franc came under pressure again. Matters came to a head in August 1993 with a widening of the ERM bands – a huge defeat for the convergists. These crises exposed how the Euro-convergists and central bankers had quite lost touch with reality. The French in particular, suspecting an Anglo-Saxon speculators' plot, talked of the re-imposition of capital controls to prevent future attack, a Canute-like response to the explosive growth in cross-border capital flows. In any event attempts at monetary convergence are doomed to fail without underlying economic convergence. Thus it was that the ERM brought a unique and systematic transfer of huge sums, not from rich area to poor, but from taxpayers to foreign currency dealers and investors. In the wake of the crisis came official statements reaffirming commitment to economic and monetary union. Of any recognition of the underlying problems of Europe's economies the politicians showed little sign. The key concern was to get the convergence programme back on track. In Britain the convergence Establishment was unrepentent to the last. They peddled their advice, and their appalling analysis, to the very end.

Meanwhile Germany, facing, according to finance minister Theo Waigel, its worst crisis since the war, is experiencing a painful fiscal and corporate retrenchment. All areas of government spending were to come under review. In 1994 insurance contributions will rise 1.8 per cent to almost 20 per cent, while higher statutory nursing-insurance will raise employers' costs further. These measures will impose an additional DM 38 billion, worsening Germany's competitiveness. A huge labour shake-out is under way.

Jacques Delors' solution to the EC's problems was predictable, if breathtaking. He called for a huge increase in EC spending on transport, electronics infrastructure and common information systems, costing £33 billion a year and financed, presumably, by raising the very taxes and costs and interest rates that lie at the heart of Eurosclerosis. Continental leaders have yet to show that they have grasped the magnitude of the challenge arising from world-wide cost restructuring and the drive to productivity. The more they shrink from doing so the more notably Europe's economies will underperform and the longer its unemployment queues will grow.

Notes

1. Deutsche Bank Economic Research, 1993.

2. Holger Schmieding, *The End of the German Miracle? Germany's Economic Prospects in Historical Perspective*, Merrill Lynch, December 15 1993, p. 2.

3. *Growth, Competitiveness and Employment in the European Community*, HM Treasury and Department of Employment, July 1993, p. 2.

4. *Financial Times*, August 28 1993.

5. *Growth, Competitiveness and Employment in the European Community*, Treasury/Dept. of Employment, 1993, p. 6.

6. 'Last Summer's Currency Crisis' in *Central Banking*, vol. III, no. 3, Winter 1992-93, ed. Robert Pringle, p. 10.

TABLE 9.1
GERMANY: FROM LEADER TO LAGGARD

West German Real GDP Growth vs. Selected Economies[*]

	1950-60	1960-73	1973-1980	1980-1990
West Germany	8.2	4.4	2.2	1.9
France	4.6	5.6	2.8	2.1
Italy	5.6	5.3	2.8	2.1
United Kingdom	2.8	3.1	0.9	2.7
United States	3.3	4.0	2.1	3.0
Japan	8.8	9.6	3.7	4.2

[*] Average annual growth rate in percentage GNP for US and Japan.

Source: Giersch, Paque, Schmieding (1992) quoted in *The End of the Economic Miracle? Germany's Economic Prospects in Historical Perspective*, Merrill Lynch, December 1993.

TABLE 9.2
PUBLIC DEBT/GDP

(%, OECD 1994 forecasts)	
Belgium	142
Italy	116
Ireland	93
Greece	91
Netherlands	81
Denmark	68
Germany[*]	64
France	61
Spain	59
UK	53

[*] including Treuhand & PO

Source: OECD.

TABLE 9.3

TOTAL LABOUR COSTS PER HOUR, 1992

Wage and non-wage costs (US = 100)

	United States	Japan	European Community *
Wage	77	87	76
Non-wage	23	24	24

* EC total = 120 per cent of US.

Source: US Bureau of Labor Statistics.

TABLE 9.4

LONG TERM UNEMPLOYED, 1991

percentage of total unemployment

country	%
United States	6
Japan	17
European Community	46

Source: OECD.

TABLE 9.5

WORLD LABOUR COSTS IN MANUFACTURING

country	1993 forecast cost ($ per hour)	ranking
West Germany	24.87	1
Norway	21.90	2
Switzerland	21.64	3
Belgium	21.00	4
Netherlands	19.83	5
Austria	19.26	6
Denmark	19.21	7
Sweden	18.30	8

[continued overleaf]

country	1993 forecast cost ($ per hour)	ranking
Former DDR	17.30	9
Japan	16.91	10
United States	16.40	11
France	16.26	12
Finland	15.36	13
Italy	14.82	14
Australia	12.91	15
United Kingdom	12.37	16
Ireland	11.88	17
Spain	11.73	18
New Zealand	8.19	19
Taiwan	5.46	20
Singapore	5.12	21
South Korea	4.93	22
Portugal	4.63	23
Hong Kong	4.21	24
Brazil	2.68	25
Mexico	2.41	26
Hungary	1.82	27
Malaysia	1.80	28
Poland	1.40	29
Czechoslovakia	1.14	30
Thailand	0.71	31
Rumania	0.68	32
Philippines	0.68	33
Bulgaria	0.63	34
China	0.44	35
Yugoslavia/Serbia	0.40	36
Indonesia	0.28	37
Russia/former SU	0.02	38

Source: DRI McGraw-Hill, Morgan Stanley Research.

TABLE 9.6
HOW EUROPE COMPARES
Percentage change from previous period

	1992	1993	1994
TRAILING ON OUTPUT ...			
United States	2.1	2.6	3.1
Japan	1.3	1.0	3.3
Germany	2.0	−1.9	1.4
OECD Europe	1.0	−0.3	1.8
Total OECD	1.5	1.2	2.7
... HIGHEST INFLATION ...			
United States	2.6	2.6	2.4
Japan	1.8	1.6	1.7
Germany	5.4	4.9	3.1
OECD Europe	4.9	4.1	3.9
Total OECD	3.3	3.0	2.8
... HIGHEST UNEMPLOYMENT ...			
% of labour force			
United States	7.4	7.0	6.5
Japan	2.2	2.5	2.6
Germany	7.7	10.1	11.3
OECD Europe	9.9	11.4	11.9
Total OECD	7.9	8.5	8.6
... HIGHEST BUDGET DEFICIT ...			
% of GDP			
United States	−4.7	−3.8	−2.9
Japan	1.8	0.1	−0.1
Germany	−2.8	−4.1	−4.1
OECD Europe	−6.0	−7.1	−6.6
Total OECD	−3.8	−4.2	−3.6

[continued overleaf]

	1992	1993	1994
... AND TRADE DEFICIT			
% of GDP			
United States	−1.0	−1.3	−1.4
Japan	3.2	3.3	3.3
Germany	−1.3	−1.5	−1.5
OECD Europe	−0.8	−0.8	−0.7
Total OECD	−0.2	−0.2	−0.1

Source: OECD Secretariat estimates, seasonally adjusted annual rates, German data for the whole of Germany.

10

White-knuckle-ride Economics

I don't make jokes – I just watch the government and report the facts.

Will Rogers

Of all the contributions to Britain's collapse of self-confidence and scramble for solution in convergence with Europe, repeated domestic economic policy failure has been the most insidious. Britain's formidable trade and budget deficits of the 1990s reach back over many years, and are testimony to the damage inflicted by successive 'quick-fix' cures that only added to the problem. The deficits now need to be addressed and rectified if there is to be any prospect of a Britain beyond Europe.

In 1990-93 Britain did not so much pass through a crisis as experience a recurrence of a condition evident since the late 1950s: a structural imbalance between investment and consumption. Failure to redress this imbalance led to a bewildering series of policy changes, U-turns and grasping at short-term solutions, all of which have contributed to a progressive weakening of the British economy and the British state, and intensified the pressure for integration with Europe.

Since the 1960s successive governments have sought to achieve three fundamental objectives: price stability, economic growth and control of public expenditure. Yet Britain was to experience the highest rate of price increases this century. On growth, she was to lag behind her competitors for most of the period, with every domestic consumer boom smashing into a balance-of-payments crisis. On public expenditure the imperative of control buckled under a political system which thrived on ever-greater auctions of public benefits and expanding welfarism.

Only once, in the mid-1980s, and helped by the endowment of North Sea oil and the proceeds of privatisations, did it appear that these three objectives were simultaneously being met. But the achievement was short-lived. Britain swung into a record balance-of-payments deficit and the economy went on to suffer its longest recession since the 1930s.

Over the years no effort has been spared – and many ministerial careers, if not lives, have been ruined – in trying to achieve success in these fundamental areas of policy. Time and again one is struck by the depth and ferocity of the conflict between the paramountcy of these objectives and the political pressures that worked to defeat their achievement.

In this the longer-term interests and well-being of the British people were to be sacrificed by their politicians for short-term electoral advantage. The result is a political economy that has been numbed by failure and drained of confidence. Britain is no nearer, either domestically or externally, to a state of viability. As the economy entered 1994, there were two formidable constraints on growth: a huge programme of tax increases to bring the budget deficit under control, and a problematic current-account deficit. Normally during a recession Britain's balance of payments goes into surplus as consumer spending on imports is reined in. But the 1990-92 recession brought only a reduction in the trade deficit before it began to worsen in 1992 and 1993. Manufacturing exports were struggling to make headway in Europe and the red line of Britain's visible trade deficit remained bogged down in the terrain it had occupied for much of the 1970s.

Meanwhile on the public finances the gap between state expenditure and income was bigger than ever despite a windfall benefit of more than £100 billion from North Sea oil and privatisations. The manufacturing base has continued to shrink and the state welfare system has swollen to an annual budget of £80 billion. The notion that higher public expenditure would alleviate social deprivation and contribute to economic growth took a long time to die. In the thirty years to 1993 public expenditure grew steadily in real, after-inflation terms, by 58 per cent. Yet for every deprivation alleviated, two more seemed to spring up.

These years were also characterised by dramatic policy convulsions and somersaults so that by the 1990s the British economy had come to resemble the after-effects of a white-knuckle ride. During this roller-coaster a commitment to full employment was embraced, and then abandoned; monetary theory and practice adopted, and then discarded; pay norms and standstills and freezes adopted, and then discarded; a model system for controlling public expenditure adopted, and then abandoned; the commitment to fixed exchange rates adhered to, and then abandoned (twice round this track); the belief that governments could 'create' economic growth adopted, and then abandoned; and, throughout all this, the expansion of one of the most costly and extensive social security systems, embodying rights over duties, in the world.

Examining economic behaviour over the years 1964 to 1985, Treasury official Peter Browning in an outstanding analysis listed the main policy failures as: Failure to reconcile a growth plan with the realities of the balance of payments; the dash for growth; the failure to control public expenditure; the inability to forecast the Public Sector Borrowing Requirement; the failure to operate sustainable credit policy and monetary policy. We had Bank Rate, Minimum Lending Rate with formula, without formula, abandoned, then re-instated; special deposits and supplementary deposits; and the failure to handle sterling crises.[1]

Most telling of all, Britain failed to secure what was required most to survive as a sovereign country: a powerful export-oriented productive base. This was the result of a progressive fiscal laxity over many years, fuelled by an electoral system of competing parcels of benefits which steadily increased consumption over investment. As a proportion of the economy's gross domestic product, personal disposable income is now at a post-war high, while the share of private investment is at a 40-year low.

The 1960s

The 1960s were haunted by balance-of-payments crises and fears of devaluation. The decade began with commitments to low inflation and low unemployment. But inflation rose by 40 per cent and unemployment doubled.

The principal concern in the early 1960s was the balance of payments. As early as 1961 a deteriorating trade balance caused by a consumer boom sucking in imported manufactured goods sparked movements out of sterling. Attempts at long-range planning or more systematic controls of public expenditure failed to make an impact. The Plowden system of public spending control, introduced in 1961, was to prove ineffective as inflation took hold.

The economic 'event' of the decade was the autumn 1967 financial crisis and devaluation. It was preceded by three warning tremors – October 1964, September 1965 and the summer of 1966. All were triggered by balance of payments pressure. All required resort to the International Monetary Fund or central bank loans. Continuing resort to deflationary measures to stave off devaluation made a nonsense of the work of the Department of Economic Affairs set up to promote economic growth, and of the National Plan – abandoned after eleven months. Throughout 1967 there was further resort to international bank loans to defend sterling, but in November the pound was devalued by 14.3 per cent (to $2.40). There was a credit squeeze and the IMF was asked for a standby credit of $1.4 billion. Some $3 billion in total was raised from central banks.

The 1967 devaluation marked the failure of attempts to massage higher growth. Alec Cairncross concluded:

> At some stage in the 1960s, almost regardless of government policy, devaluation was perhaps inevitable. In the 18 years since the devaluation of 1949, the competitive power of British industry had failed to keep pace with that of other industrialised countries and a proneness to inflation developed that was difficult to control. What was not inevitable was that devaluation would restore competitive power and external balance.[2]

Another sterling crisis arose towards the end of 1968. Britain was required to negotiate foreign borrowings, this time amounting to $8 billion. Devaluation was reckoned to have benefited the balance of payments by £700 million in three years.

But there was an inflationary price. Between 1968 and 1970 consumer prices rose by almost 20 per cent. Inflation, which was running at 2.8 per cent in 1967 rose to 8.5 per cent in 1970 and continued at 8 per cent in 1971. Nor was it to arrest the decline in Britain's share of world trade in manufactures. This fell over the decade from 16.5 per cent to 10.8 per cent. During the decade labour costs rose 32 per cent, the highest in the OECD countries.

The 1970s

The 1970s marked the high tide of Keynesian demand management and the belief that government and public expenditure could engineer prosperity. It was also a decade in which Britain became chronically addicted to inflation. In 1970 the Chancellor of the new Conservative government, Anthony Barber, decided to ride the tiger of 'dash for growth' economics in a way no previous Chancellor had done. In this he was supported by the City, the then influential National Institute for Economic and Social Research and the economics establishment. It was to prove one of the most ruinous episodes in post-war economic management. Taxes were cut throughout 1970-72 and monetary policy loosened. But increased pressure of demand as the economy approached capacity-working fuelled inflation. Hourly wage rates rose by 13 per cent in each of the two years 1971-72, triggering a renewed attempt at incomes policy. The government was driven back to incomes controls to tame the tiger. In February 1974, during the miners' strike, the Heath government fell.

By the summer of 1975 retail prices were rising at an annual rate of 27 per cent and the Public Sector Borrowing Requirement had soared to £12 billion. The following year interest rates soared, from a low of 9 per cent in March to a peak of 15 per cent in October. Meanwhile unemployment, far from being 'cured' by inflation, climbed over one million in 1976 and remained at 1.2 million through 1977 and 1978. Attempts to control public expenditure during 1974 and 1975 failed through a combination of political opposition and runaway inflation. Confidence within both industry and the markets plummeted. Few economies could have achieved the simultaneous combination of zero growth, rapid inflation, substantial unemployment and a current-account deficit.

In the ensuing crisis Britain applied for a further IMF loan of $3.9 billion. The negotiations resulted in plans to cut the PSBR and public expenditure and to target the growth in Domestic Credit Expansion. Boosted by the rising flow of North Sea oil the balance of payments went into surplus in 1977 – the first time since 1972. But confidence began to weaken on worries about the money supply, a faltering in the balance of payments and a sharp rise in pay rises. In August 1978 the government announced a pay policy to limit rises to 5 per cent. The result was public sector strikes, the winter of discontent – and the election of a Conservative government under Margaret Thatcher.

Achievements and illusions: the 1980s

For the first time in a generation it looked as if Britain, now enjoying massive North Sea oil revenues, could break free from the constraints of the past twenty years, cut personal tax and build a new platform for economic growth. North Sea oil would be the springboard. The Thatcher government of 1979 embarked on a radical programme of trade-union reform, government spending control, reductions in personal tax and control of inflation through bearing down on the money supply.

The monetary squeeze, while bringing a sharp fall in inflation, cut an unintentionally severe swathe through manufacturing capacity. The recession of 1980-81 traumatised industry. In 1984 Chancellor Nigel Lawson called for spending cuts of £500 million but got only half of this. According to Sir Leo Pliatsky, 'the Treasury gave up, for practical purposes, the attempt to cut total expenditure, but adopted a new strategy of stabilising it in real terms'.[3] By January 1985 a further bout of dollar strength threatened to take the pound down to a 1:1 parity with the dollar. Interest rates were raised to 14 per cent. The Chancellor had embarked upon a policy that was to have implications far beyond a deepening and ultimately fatal rift with the Prime Minister: an unspoken tracking of the Deutschemark.

It paved the way for the abandonment of the belief in reliance on the markets, the return to fixed exchange rates, the entry of sterling into the Exchange Rate Mechanism and the signing by Britain of the Maastricht Treaty. Such clandestine initiation of policy, with huge national implications, was remarkable, had it not been for the fact that it effectively marked a collapse of faith in Britain's ability to beat inflation on her own.

Helped by privatisation receipts and rising Corporation Tax revenues, Britain by March of 1988 was now enjoying a Public Sector Debt Repayment, encouraging the Chancellor to cut personal tax further. The effect was to accelerate a runaway consumer boom. Bank and building society lending jumped by 24 per cent and house prices by 23 per cent. Broad money was now rising by 17.6 per cent a year. The Treasury had seriously under-estimated the boom, and the brakes, belatedly, began to be applied. Lawson resigned in October 1989, the trigger being an article by the Prime Minister's economic adviser Professor Alan Walters in which he wrote:

> The pressure from Europe and the British Establishment to conform and join the ERM has been enormous. But the arguments have never attained even a minimum level of plausibility. My advice has been for Britain to retain its system of flexible exchange rates and to stay out of the present arrangements of the ERM. So far Mrs Thatcher has concurred ... It would not be in Britain's, or, I believe, Europe's interest, to join the present half-baked system.[4]

In October 1990, John Major took Britain into the ERM at the central rate of DM 2.95. By now Britain was heading for recession, the consequence of a lending-fuelled consumer boom which forced inflation back up to almost 10 per cent and interest rates up to 15 per cent.

For a time the 1980s was seen by many as a decade which had 'saved' the British economy, or at least showed what Britain was capable of. Trade-union reform was long overdue, the collapse of the 1984-85 miners' strike was to mark a turning-point in labour relations, and from the mid-1980s there was an altogether changed climate within industry, with a marked reduction in costs and improvement in productivity. There was continuous expansion from 1982 and a bigger rise in output than in any previous decade.

But for the public finances the gains were brief. The first three years of the 1990s were to see the re-emergence of a colossal budget deficit and a spiralling trade deficit, followed by £30 billion of tax increases announced in the Lamont and Clarke budgets of 1993. The 1980s presented a unique opportunity by virtue of North Sea oil and a government committed to restore discipline over the public finances. What went wrong?

First, on the principal goal of economic policy, reduction of inflation, success proved to be short-lived – and the price of even temporary advantage colossal. The 1980s proved to be one of the most inflationary decades of post-war Britain: prices more than doubled. In the assessment of Christopher Huhne:

The economy was lifted by a balloon of personal credit which expanded from a mere £90.5 billion at the end of 1980 to more than £328 billion in 1988. Individuals' liabilities – their mortgages, personal bank loans, credit card debts and so on – rose from 45 per cent of pre-tax incomes at the beginning of the decade to more than 85 per cent in 1988. Never have so many borrowed so much so quickly.[5]

It was not the Howe and Lawson budgets of the early and mid-1980s that were to break the psychology of inflation and instil a national discipline, but the recession and debt deflation of 1990-92.

A second characteristic of the decade was high unemployment. It rose to at least five times the highest level in the 1960s, peaking in 1986 at 3.1 million (11.1 per cent of the workforce). For seven of the ten years it was over two million. The persistence of high unemployment reflected a third, more worrying characteristic of the 1980s: the continuing collapse of Britain's manufacturing base. Over the decade two million jobs were lost in manufacturing, 24 per cent of its total workforce, as capacity was taken out. In 1965 the sector accounted for forty jobs in every 100. By the 1990s this had fallen to 22 in every 100. Instead of the gains of North Sea oil being used to secure a new stream of export earnings there was an unprecedented consumer boom: consumer spending rose from 59 per cent of GDP in 1979 to 66 per cent in 1990.

A fourth, related legacy of the 1980s was a chronic structural balance-of-payments deficit. While exports improved there was an explosion in imports, despite a continuing and at times severe devaluation. Between 1980 and 1990 imports rose by almost £60 billion (at constant 1985 prices), double the increase of any previous decade. Throughout the early 1980s there was a belief that the balance of payments had ceased to matter, partly as a result of North Sea oil and partly through a belief, articulated by Lawson, that imbalances in trade in manufactured goods mattered little in the brave new world of cross-border capital flows.

By 1989 imports of manufactures accounted for nearly 80 per cent of all imports and exceeded exports of manufactured goods by 25 per cent. In 1980 Britain had a surplus on non-oil trade of just over £1 billion. By 1989 this had swung into a deficit of £25 billion. The overall current-account balance swung from a surplus of £2.8 billion in 1980 to a deficit of £17 billion by 1990, the £44 billion contribution from North Sea oil effectively dissipated in a consumer boom fuelled by tax cuts.

Finally, what of the other two goals of government policy: the reduction in taxation and the restoration of sound public finance? Direct taxes came down significantly but there was no relief from the growth of the tax burden overall. Taxes and National Insurance contributions as a percentage of GDP stood at 34.75 per cent in the year before the Conservatives took office. By the time the Lamont and Clarke tax increases are fully implemented in 1997-98 the figure will be up to 38 per cent, more than wiping out the gains of the 1980s and raising the total tax burden to a level substantially higher than that ever experienced under a Labour government.

A similar pattern of short-lived improvement followed by relapse could be seen in public expenditure. Between 1978-79 and 1988-89 general government spending fell from 44 per cent of GDP to 39.25 per cent. But the ratio was to climb back to 44.75 per cent in 1992-93 and rise further to 45 per cent in 1993-94. In cash terms general government spending including privatisation receipts totalled just under £180 billion. By 1993-94 it had soared to £281 billion, with huge increases in spending on health, social security, local government expenditure and education.

Set against this inexorable advance, the revenues from North Sea oil and privatisations were soon more than dissipated, with a final round of tax cuts as these windfall benefits fell to a trickle making a budgetary crisis only a matter of time.

Cumulative damage

More damaging than the opportunity foregone of the 1980s was the cumulative deterioration caused by a series of recessions following on domestically fuelled overruns in consumer demand. The recession of 1979-81 inflicted severe long-term damage on Britain's industrial base. Between 1980 and 1983 capacity dropped by some 16 per cent. The renewed loss of capacity in the 1990-92 recession more than wiped out the gains of the 1980s. The decade which should have seen new export industries to replace the declining earnings from North Sea oil saw instead the loss of around one-seventh of manufacturing capacity. The result is that, in any ensuing recovery, capacity constraint – and consequently balance-of-payments constraint – is felt at an ever earlier stage of recovery.

Economic cycles are inevitable. But what is worrying about the British experience is the extent to which the cycles have grown in amplitude: as UBS economist Bill Martin put it, 'Lawson out-boomed Barber; Major out-slumped Howe.'[6]

In the 1950s and 60s recessions were characterised by slow-downs in growth rather than absolute falls in output. By contrast the recessions of 1974-75, 1980-81 and 1990-92 were each marked by sharp falls in output. A similar trend of long-term deterioration can be seen in unemployment. In the early 1950s it stood at 1 per cent of the workforce. By 1993 it peaked at 10.5 per cent. Far from the swings diminishing in amplitude they have increased. After each downturn the recorded peak in unemployment has been higher than at the previous peak; and after each upturn the trough has been deeper than the previous trough.

It was in recognition of Britain's pronounced predeliction for the good times 'on tick' that Kenneth Clarke declared soon after taking on the Chancellorship in 1993 that he wanted a decade of recovery 'driven by investment and exports not consumption, by the private sector, not the state'. The nature of the change required was well understood by him, even if the magnitude had still to be grasped.

The balance of payments swing has been dramatic. In the mid-1960s manufactured goods represented only 44 per cent of imports but 84 per cent of exports. By the mid-1980s they still accounted for nearly 75 per cent of exports, but they also comprised 73 per cent of imports. In 1950, imports of manufactures equalled only 4 per cent of GDP. By 1991 they had reached 18.5 per cent.

The failure of the state to maintain price stability has been principally responsible for the volatility both in interest rates and in fiscal policy, which in turn brought a weakening of Britain's industrial base. Between 1959 and 1975 inflation swung from 1 per cent to a peak of 24 per cent. It then fell, only to rise back to 22 per cent in 1980 before falling to under 2 per cent in 1993. Interest rates have veered as a consequence between extremes of 5 per cent and 17 per cent. Between 1960 and 1990 base rate or Minimum Lending Rate has changed no less than 194 times. This compares with 31 in the period 1930-50. Between 1933 and 1938 there was no change whatever in Bank Rate, which was steady at 2 per cent. In 1988 alone, base rate changed on 16 occasions, veering between 7.5 per cent and 13 per cent.

This instability had insidiously destructive effects for Britain. It has biased investors in favour of projects with short-term returns. According to Dr Walter Eltis, UK firms have been more vulnerable to price instability and interest rate shocks because the surplus of average profitability over interest has been much less than in Germany and Japan.[7]

More dramatically, it has biased lending and investment portfolios towards property, both in the company and the personal sector. The billions of pounds poured into residential property because of its attractions as an inflation-hedge represent the single most dramatic distortion of savings, with the productive sector consequently deprived of capital that would otherwise have been available at lower cost and in greater amounts. This distortion was magnified by government subsidy, by way of tax relief on mortgage interest and direct subsidy to reduce local taxes through local authority support grants, which are the second largest central government cost. In the ten years 1979-89 housing as a proportion of personal wealth rose from 39.5 per cent to 42 per cent, helped by the subvention of mortgage interest relief which rose from £2 billion in 1980 to £7 billion by the end of the decade.

Meanwhile, as the productive base of the economy has shrunk, welfare spending has soared, unrelated to state revenues and the fluctuations in the real economy. Since 1949 welfare spending has risen eightfold in real terms and now accounts for almost 13 per cent of GDP. A recurring problem has been how to effect restraint and control over public goods and services in a democratic market place where the political process constantly bids up demand for services and 'resources'. Every attempt to exercise restraint is attacked as 'massive spending cuts', and where reductions are made they are often in the areas critical for longer-term break-out and recovery. How self-defeating, but all-too-predictable, that while welfare spending is budgeted to increase to even higher levels between 1993-94 and 1996-97, it is the Department of Trade and Industry that has to bear the brunt of the cuts, with its budget more than halved over this period, from £3.6 billion to £1.4 billion.

Given that the politicians' stock-in-trade is more public goods and spending, it is hard to see how more realistic public attitudes can be encouraged except through a radical change in culture. To date Britain has not found a way of reconciling the permanent discipline of low inflation and public expenditure restraint on government and political behaviour. Indeed the political culture has worked to conceal from the public the full nature and extent of Britain's economic predicament.

The magnitude of the task now required to address the deep structural problems of the British economy will require a radical change in public thinking. Britain's exit from the ERM and the subsequent sharp falls in interest rates helped build a base for recovery. But there is no agreement on how it will bear up under the impact of three successive years of tax increases and whether, as some maintain, inflation has been permanently beaten.

That such a reckoning is seen as inevitable is not through some sudden change of circumstance or unexpected crisis of events. Britain has not come to this by accident but by a long and problematic past, a moment of truth a generation in the making.

Notes

1. Peter Browning, *The Treasury and Economic Policy, 1964-1985*, 1986, pp. 350-3.

2. Alec Cairncross, *The British Economy since 1945*, 1992.

3. Sir Leo Pliatsky, *Paying and Choosing*.

4. Sir Alan Walters, *Financial Times*, October 18 1989.

5. Christopher Huhne, *Real World Economics*, 1991, p. 158.

6. Bill Martin, *Beyond Our Ken*, Economic Research Bulletin, UBS, November 1993.

7. Dr Walter Eltis, *The Financial Foundations of Industrial Success*, Esmée Fairbairn Lecture, November 1992.

TABLE 10.1
THE RISE OF THE TAX BURDEN

Taxes, social security contributions and community charge as a
percentage of non-North Sea GDP.

1965-66	31.75
1966-67	32.5
1967-68	34.0
1968-69	35.75
1969-70	37.5
1970-71	37.0
1971-72	35.25
1972-73	33.0
1973-74	33.75
1974-75	36.25
1975-76	36.75
1976-77	36.5
1977-78	35.5
1978-79	34.75
1979-80	35.5
1980-81	36.5
1981-82	39.25
1982-83	38.5
1983-84	38.25
1984-85	38.35
1985-86	37.25
1986-87	37.75
1987-88	38.0
1988-89	37.35
1989-90	37.0
1990-91	37.0
1991-92	36.25
1992-93	35.0
1993-94	34.25

[continued overleaf]

Taxes, social security contributions and community charge as a percentage of non-North Sea GDP.

1994-95 (e)	35.5
1995-96 (e)	37.0
1996-97 (e)	37.5
1997-98 (e)	38.0
1998-99 (e)	38.5

(e) = FSBR estimates.

Source: Financial Statement and Budget Report 1994-95. HM Treasury, November 1994.

TABLE 10.2
HOW SPENDING HAS RISEN

General government expenditure including privatisation proceeds (£bn)

1978-79	75.0
1979-80	90.0
1980-81	108.6
1981-82	120.5
1982-83	132.7
1983-84	140.4
1984-85	150.8
1985-86	158.5
1986-87	164.8
1987-88	173.2
1988-89	179.8
1989-90	200.8
1990-91	218.1
1991-92	236.2

General government expenditure including privatisation proceeds
(£bn)

1992-93	261.1
1993-94	280.7
1994-95 (e)	291.8
1995-96 (e)	312.1
1996-97 (e)	324.2

(e) = FSBR estimates.

Source: Financial Statement and Budget Report, 1994-95. HM
Treasury, November 1993.

TABLE 10.3
SHARE OF MANUFACTURED IMPORTS IN GDP

	Level %	Increase over previous decade
1950	3.9	—
1960	5.8	1.9
1970	10.3	4.5
1980	15.4	5.1
1990	20.4	5.0

Source: Midland Global Markets.

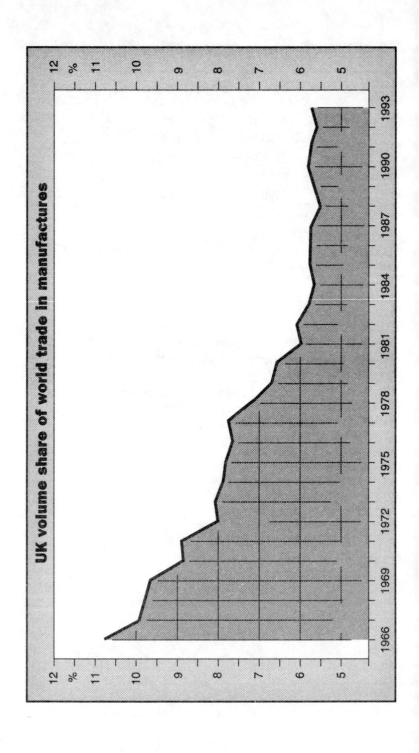

UK volume share of world trade in manufactures

11

Debt and the Dependency Machine

The State, in organising security, should not stifle incentive, opportunity, responsibility: in establishing a national minimum, it should leave room and encouragement for voluntary action by each individual.

William Beveridge, Social Security and
Allied Services, Cmd. 6404, 1942

From the moment Chancellor Kenneth Clarke presented his budget in November 1993, the stock market began one of its strongest rallies since the champagne days of the 1980s. Clarke was seen to have lifted the single greatest burden on the UK economy: he had made the budget deficit dissolve before disbelieving eyes: confident Treasury projections showed the PSBR melting from £50 billion to just £2 billion over five years. 'Britain's recovery', Clarke declared, 'can only be maintained if we tackle the budget deficit now. In my opinion the budget must sort out the problem of public borrowing once and for all.'

But Clarke's budget had not so much removed the burden as shifted it. His package had added a further £13 billion of tax increases on top of an existing £17 billion programme of rises left by his predecessor Norman Lamont, while public expenditure, in particular welfare spending, was projected to rise to even greater heights.

Within a month share prices in London had risen 10 per cent in salute, entering 1994 at an all-time high. In the strange and ghostly terrain between the announcement of these massive tax increases and their implementation, the markets became convinced that the economy would gather pace and that the impact of three successive years of rising tax would be absorbed by consumers who would soon adjust to a tax regime more penal than in the era of Labour's Denis Healey.

For the government it was as much a humiliation as a triumph. A year earlier it had fought an election with an economic programme resting on two pillars. The first was Britain's continued membership of the ERM. This was kicked away within five months of taking office. The second was a commitment to low taxation. Not only did the two 1993 budgets demolish that commitment, they would also sweep away the aggregate falls in tax achieved by the three Thatcher administrations and impose an overall tax take on the economy higher than any imposed by a Labour government. The Major administration did not so much lead Britain into recovery: it somersaulted.

But in the euphoria of early 1994 the point that investors had overlooked was that the curtailment in borrowing had left untouched the prime engine of public expenditure growth: Britain's colossal welfare machine, whose budget would continue to grow.

The central argument within the Treasury in the approach to the high tax budgets of 1993 was whether the explosion in government borrowing was cyclical – caused by recession – which would correct itself as recovery gathered pace; or structural – caused by a secular, systemic rise in government expenditure irrespective of the state of the underlying economy – which would require corrective action by way of spending cuts or tax increases.

A subsidiary issue then came to the fore: to the extent that fiscal action was required, how much should be borne by public expenditure cuts and how much by tax increases, bearing in mind the fragile nature of the recovery, the overhang of household debt from the 1980s and the low level of consumer confidence?

The plunge into massive borrowing – from a small budget surplus in 1990-91 to a borrowing requirement of 8 per cent of GDP in 1993-94 – was slow to emerge as a public issue. Throughout 1991 and early 1992 the Treasury was dismissive of any notion that there was a budgetary 'problem' – maintaining, particularly through the 1991 Autumn Statement, that government spending as a share of the national income was not materially out of line with the position during the Thatcher years.

The assertion that there was 'no problem' on expenditure

flowed from a belief that the deterioration in the public finances was primarily due to recession. The Treasury orthodoxy was that the downturn in activity had simultaneously brought a fall in receipts from income and corporation tax and a rise in public expenditure on 'cyclical' social security as unemployment rose.

However, the scale of the deterioration pointed to problems at the heart of government more serious than cyclical downturn and which had been building long before the onset of the 1990-92 recession. Four Conservative administrations since 1979 had been returned on a platform of less government, lower tax, entrepreneurial self-reliance, a clampdown on government spending and an end to the dependency culture. Britain could reasonably have expected at the end of these fourteen years at least a check on the growth of government, a reduction in the budget deficit as a percentage of GDP and a containment of public spending in line with the growth of the economy. It was to be disappointed in all of these.

The period since 1979 can be divided into three phases. In the first of these, covering the years 1979-80 to 1981-82, general government spending rose by 2.3 per cent a year in real terms (that is, after allowing for inflation), a slowdown on the 3.7 per cent average for the preceding years 1963 to 1987. The second lasted between 1982-83 and 1987-88. During this, government spending rose in real terms by just 0.6 per cent. But in the third phase, from 1988-89 to 1992-93, spending climbed again, by an average annual rate of 3.1 per cent.[1]

Thus, throughout the long span of Conservative government, public spending continued to rise in real terms, the growth moderating in the central span but accelerating markedly over the later years. It rose by a total of 13 per cent in real terms over this latter period, with nearly all government programmes showing increases, while GDP fell. It was not recession *per se*, but rather a trend of underlying public-expenditure accelera-tion aggravated by recession that led to a budget deficit of 8 per cent of GDP. This was the highest ever recorded in a period of Conservative administration and the opposite of the result that the party manifestos had promised. Even so, it did not at first create alarm, or even censure. The Britain that had voted for prudent control of the public finances was the same Britain that wanted a 'softer' face of Thatcherism – though it could not discern the tax implications that lay behind her successor's smile (nor, more worryingly perhaps, did he).

Britain wanted less government, but more public infrastructure spending; less tax, but more subsidies to soften reform of the rating system; a less state-reliant society but more dependants; carefully targeted spending, but ever greater 'resources' for health and education. Above all, it wanted a welfare system not only maintained in real terms but expanded. Thus, it was not only a weak and vapid government that had been 'rumbled' by the recession, but also a deep ambiguity that ran to the heart of national attitudes on what government should, and should not, do. We wanted continence and chastity, but in the way that St Augustine wanted chastity: not yet!

Throughout the rapid slide into deficit, belief in the ability of government to balance the budget, if not from one year to another, then at least over the span of the economic cycle (from peak to peak) at first remained intact. Indeed it was this analysis that informed the 1991 and 1992 budgets and played a large part in the decision in the 1993 budget to defer the bulk of planned tax increases into 1994-95, so as to allow the benign zephyrs of recovery to waft through the national accounts and 'melt' the deficit away. In retrospect the period 1989-93 must be seen as one of the worst periods of post-war economic management and on a par with the Barber-Heath dash for growth in the early 1970s.

But to admit that there was any explanation of the budgetary collapse other than recession would have been to question government stewardship of the public finances before 1990 and open the way for a re-examination of the 1980s. The period up to 1988 was being allowed to pass into public mythology as a golden era of fiscal rectitude. Which government minister would admit any fundamental crack in this icon? And which Treasury mandarin would so dare admit?

Complacency on the government accounts and public expenditure permeated the Major administration from the outset. Not only was it reluctant to admit that the growth of public expenditure was a problem, but it also proceeded on a course of large discretionary increases in spending. Thus, outside social security, spending on health in the four years 1992-93 rose by more than 4 per cent in real terms; on housing by almost 10 per cent; on law and order by 6 per cent. Transitional relief to ease the switch from Poll Tax to Council Tax in 1992-93 alone cost £6.6 billion.[2] Moreover during the period between 1988-89 and 1992-93 spending by 'other' departments – transport, the Foreign and Commonwealth Office, the Home Office, education and Scotland and Wales – soared. One struggles to grasp how, in an era of supposed public expenditure control, the aggregate £29 billion budget of these departments was allowed to rise by £21 billion or 72 per cent in four years.

What distinguished the early 1990s was not some new or unprecedented change of policy but the acceleration of trends evident in the public finances for many years. These reflected in part the remorseless rise in voter expectations, partly the rise in the power and effectiveness of lobbies and special interest groups. But they also mirrored wider social changes and the inherent tendency of government itself to expand and lay claim to ever more of the nation's resources. It took the arrival of a record budget deficit to force the Treasury to act. The manner of Norman Lamont in this exercise was akin to that of a manager of a high-security bank who had proudly claimed that his premises were burglar-proof, while slowly realising that the vaults had been stripped bare by a group of well-dressed and credit-worthy men and women whose identikit pictures disturbingly resembled the government front bench.

The figures behind the spring 1993 budget blew the ground from under the cosy 'recession-to-blame' explanations of the fiscal collapse. Not only had general public spending climbed alarmingly, but far from the PSBR 'melting away' with recovery, it would still be running at £46 billion three years later unless action was taken.

The crisis in the public finances exposed two myths at the heart of government. The first was that there had been a substantial improvement in the underlying fiscal position in the 1980s. In fact the PSBR, after stripping out proceeds from North Sea oil, privatisations and council-house sales, had, far from improving, continued to deteriorate through the early 1980s, reaching 7.7 per cent of GDP in 1984-85. It fell back for four years as the economy expanded but was never eliminated as the gross figures suggested.

The emphasis on the 'cyclical' nature of the PSBR disguised the extent to which state spending behaviour failed to take account of the sharp decline in North Sea oil revenues from

1986. According to Bill Robinson, former special adviser to Norman Lamont, the large and growing revenue from North Sea oil up to 1986 enabled the government to hold taxes lower while the high exchange rate made imports cheaper. 'Thus', he was later to write:

> North Sea oil, far from being used to re-finance and re-equip British manufacturing industry, was a means of fuelling a new British economy, one that was to be driven by designer restaurants, keep-fit gymnasia and personal financial managers as thousands of manufacturing companies went to the wall.[3]

Far from taxes being raised as revenue began to fall, they were cut further. And, far from the government reining in public spending, it allowed spending to accelerate rapidly. Robinson estimated the North Sea oil revenue loss from 1986 at £12 billion.[4] An unexpected rise in Corporation Tax revenues disguised the problem for a while. But the telling error would come to light: just as this huge windfall revenue went into decline, government spending began a fatal acceleration.

Treasury explanations of the 'cyclical' budget deficit now came under question. Economist Michael Saunders at Salomon Brothers estimated that the structural component was much larger than officially admitted, at between half and two-thirds of the PSBR total. By the summer of 1993 Oxford Economic Forecasting estimated the structural element of the deficit at around £35 billion. And Bill Martin at UBS argued that, at a sustainable rate of GDP growth, pretty well all the deficit was non-cyclical. Lamont was dismissive of the controversy, saying that it didn't matter so long as action was taken to bring it down.[5] But the issue went to the heart of what action was necessary for the Treasury to take and whether the deficit could be tackled by conventional budget 'packages' at all.

The second myth at the heart of government was that the dependency culture had been decisively rolled back. But throughout the 1980s, and particularly under the Major administration, there was a substantial increase, both in the number of claimants and in the amounts being disbursed. Because these were statutory entitlements the Treasury's claim to be 'in control' of government spending carried little conviction, particularly when, even in those areas where it had discretion, expenditure, far from being reined in to make room for the extra social-security disbursements, was being expanded. Thus, by the time Kenneth Clarke became Chancellor in the spring of 1993, the reductions were far more difficult and disruptive to effect. But thus it has always been in government spending: the additions, justified at first as being only temporary, become permanent terrain.

By 1993 the social security budget had climbed to £85 billion, up from £49 billion five years earlier, making it the biggest single item in the government's spending programme. Far from declining as Treasury exponents of the 'cyclical deficit' school argued, it was forecast by the Department of Social Security to rise to more than £92 million by 1996-97. Indeed 'cyclical' social security – the component of the DSS budget that was reckoned to melt away as the recovery gathered pace – was forecast to rise from £13 billion in 1992-93 to £16 billion by 1996-97.[6]

Between 1978-79 and 1992-93, spending on social security rose in real terms by £31 billion or 67 per cent. Real spending on the sick and disabled almost trebled and spending on the elderly climbed by 40 per cent.[7] Ministers like to claim that the financial implications of spending decisions are carefully thought out and the consequences for the national accounts fully weighed. Two small examples will suffice of the unplanned and unintended consequence of the expansion of welfare provision. First, the number of single-parent families receiving supplementary benefit or income support shot from 625,000 in 1987-88 to more than 900,000 in 1992-93 and the the figure is still rising.[8]

The second involves invalidity benefit. In 1979 around 600,000 claimed invalidity benefit at a cost of £340 million. As benefits were made more generous the number of claimants shot up to 1.3 million by 1993 and the cost above £8 billion.[9] Like so many benefits it was never, of course, intended that higher payments would attract more claimants and propel numbers and costs in the way they did. Yet it was clearly forseeable that if you pay more money out to 'invalids', you create more 'invalids' to come forward and collect. Meanwhile any suggestion that the benefit be cut stood to provoke a public outcry.

Across the welfare system the numbers in receipt of state hand-outs soared. At the end of a 14-year period in which the dependency culture was to be reduced, the score was as follows: 9.9 million in receipt of state pension; 340,000 widow's benefit; 715,000 unemployment benefit; 135,000 sickness benefit; 935,000 disability living allowance; 85,000 statutory maternity pay; 5.3 million income support; 6.8 million families child benefit; 420,000 family credit; 3.1 million rent rebates; 1.2 million rent allowances and 6.6 million Community Charge Benefit.

Of the 25 major benefits on offer, the most costly are retirement pension (£24.5 billion) and child benefit (£5.5 billion). Nearly a quarter of all benefit spending is now going to people on above-average incomes. It is not hard to see why the continued existence of these universal benefits came into question. And as the benefits rose, so did the costs.

Between 1987-88 and 1992-93 administrative expenses climbed by almost two-thirds to £3.8 billion. To administer sickness and invalidity benefit costs £3.55 per week per person; income support £5.65 per week per person and sickness and unemployment benefit £9.15 per week per person. The DSS's own payroll climbed 18 per cent in three years to more than 98,000 and the pay bill from £990 million in 1987-88 to £1.5 billion in 1992-93.

Demographic factors are partly responsible. In the 1980s the number of people over 60 increased by half-a-million and the number over 75 to almost four million with attendant calls on health and other social services. But two-thirds of single parents are now dependent on means-tested benefits compared with one third a decade ago. And the size of the 'non-cyclical' social security is now vast, at 24 per cent of all government spending.

This spending did not suddenly become problematic with changes in administration or with the onset of recession. It has been rising remorselessly and without interruption in real terms for forty years. Since 1949-50 it has climbed, after inflation, more than sevenfold. To finance just one year's spending now requires a tax generation equivalent to more than 50 companies the size of British Petroleum.

The growth of the welfare and transfer system has been dramatic, far outstripping the original Beveridge ideas which passed into legislation in the late 1940s. Moreover it has grown over a period when living standards in Britain measured by such items as consumer spending, family budgets, home ownership and consumer goods have soared beyond anything imagined in the 1940s.

Beveridge has cast a lengthening shadow over social policy. The welfare machine he set in motion developed ambitions far greater than the alleviation of poverty. Writing in 1950, Richard Titmuss put his finger on the huge enlargement of the state, over and above the treatment of poverty, that Beveridge had in mind:

> No longer did concern rest on the belief that, in respect of many needs, it was proper to intervene only to assist the poor and those who were unable to pay for services of one kind or another. Instead it was increasingly regarded as a proper function or even obligation of government to ward off distress and strain among not only the poor but almost all classes of society.[10]

The Beveridge plan covered loss of income resulting from unemployment, sickness and retirement. Social assistance should be limited to a safety net to deal with emergencies and those with special needs. The scheme that came into operation in 1948 was far more generous and comprehensive than the variety of schemes it replaced.

But it was not long before a pattern emerged of 'special case' payments being consolidated into overall entitlements. At each consolidation it was hoped that a line had been drawn and the growth checked, only for 'special case' payments to spring up. In 1961 graduated pensions were introduced together with graduated contributions.

This was extended in 1966 to unemployment and sickness benefits. The elderly, sick and disabled who had never worked were brought within the social-security system. Problems also arose with National Assistance, with additional payments for special needs such as fuel or laundry. By 1966 these were being paid to six out of every ten beneficiaries. In 1966 National Assistance was replaced by Supplementary Benefit, which brought all these extra payments together.

Also embracing automatic additions for pensioners and others, the new system was designed to reduce the need for any other payments. But by 1974 more than one in three recipients were receiving extra payments from the Supplementary Benefits Commission. In 1980 these were codified and became legal entitlements. Again, while this led initially to a drop in additional payments, the pattern of continually increasing payments soon recurred.

In 1971 Family Income Supplement was introduced to help those unable to build up their contribution records. Attendance allowance was introduced to meet the extra costs faced by disabled people. In 1976 Invalid Care Allowance was introduced. A similar 'advance-consolidate-advance' pattern was evident in the fields of pensions and housing benefits. By 1985 this complex and ever-expanding system of interlocking and overlapping entitlements was costing more than £40 billion a year.

A review was undertaken to simplify the system, examine where it could be made more efficient and ensure that money was properly targeted. In this way the Conservative government hoped to slow down the social security explosion. But by 1992-93 the annual bill had leapt to £80 billion. Cyclical social security in particular was rising rapidly. More of the unemployed were in middle- and upper-income brackets with mortgage commitments which the state took on for a period. Mortgage-interest support jumped from £115 million in 1978-79 to more than £1 billion by 1992-93. One problem for the Treasury was the extent to which the take-up of unemployment benefit rose in each downturn but failed to fall, or fall by as much, when recovery arrived.

Every addition, extension and increase of the vast social-security apparatus was justified on the grounds either that it would cost the taxpayer 'only a pint of beer a week' or that the economy would soon be showing real growth and the extra cost would not be noticed. In truth, the thriving productive sector that was necessary to create jobs and generate the revenue for such state welfarism was to be debilitated by these costs. The notion that there were limits to Beveridge was a delusion. But down the slope we went. As we did so, every attempt to contain the welfare empire brought scorn from politicians who had ridden this tiger for electoral benefit. Thus did Beveridge grow into imperial welfarism.

Getting to grips with the social security budget requires a change in thinking about welfare provision that has dominated the post-war era. There is no doubt that the present system is indiscriminately targeted, the costs excessive, destined to increase unless corrective action is taken, and the culture self-destructive. It works to discourage private provision and is inefficient in the relief of genuine poverty. In the discarding of voluntary agencies, it also went further than Beveridge advocated and led him to express misgiving.

The aim of social security provision should be to provide a temporary safety net for those unable to provide for themselves. It should aim as far as possible for the restoration of self-reliance. The present system has encouraged a welfare dependency the more it has grown, breeding more of the broken homes and social disadvantage it sought to alleviate. A key reason why such reform has been so difficult is the notion of a yawning black hole of deprivation that would develop if social security provision returned to the private sector or was curtailed.

This presupposes that before Beveridge, and certainly before the Lloyd George National Insurance Act, there was no system of provision and that the state pension scheme was the first collective attempt to provide for retirement.

Research by David Green of the Institute of Economic Affairs and Timothy Evans for the Adam Smith Institute has forced a re-examination of this notion. So, too, has recent work by Labour MP Frank Field. This has focused on the importance of friendly societies in pension and unemployment cover provision before the entry of the state.

Friendly societies covered the cost not only of burial but of sickness and unemployment. They were non-profit-making institutions, founded on the principles of mutual aid. They were democratically run – characteristics which have enabled Field to locate private mutuality as lying firmly within the Labour tradition. Green goes further in suggesting that the growth of state provision was actively encouraged by professional interest groups as a means of increasing fees, and by the insurance companies as a means of eliminating competition.

Before the 1911 National Insurance Act the friendly societies' social insurance and primary medical care schemes had attracted more than three-quarters of all manual workers. In 1892 the Chief Registrar of Friendly Societies testified to the Royal Commission on Labour that there were as many members of unregistered friendly societies as members of registered ones.[11]

With the number of registered friendly society members at 3.8 million, this would give a total of six million out of an industrial male population of seven million. By 1910 there were

6.6 million members of registered societies and by the 1911 Act between 9 and 9.5 million of the 12 million eventually to be covered were in insurance schemes. By the beginning of the twentieth century the total funds of the various provident institutions came to almost £400 million – the most rapid rate of increase in funds in the last years of the nineteenth century being in the friendly societies and the retail co-operatives.

As Green has emphasised and academics such as Titmuss tended to ignore, the British needed no lessons from the state in the virtues of thrift, any more than they needed the state to operate a national thrift organisation on their behalf. In particular, the working class did not require to be singled out in such a patronising manner for cradle-to-grave management of their affairs by the state, and the state did not have to 'teach' social security or 'manage' the pension contributions of millions nowhere near the poverty line. It could not hope to be as adaptive and responsive to the many differing and various needs of a growing, increasingly sophisticated and less deferential population.

And it was an unnecessary and inefficient diversion from the need to focus on those genuinely poor who could make no provision for themselves. The friendly societies fostered a spirit of mutual aid and voluntary effort without detracting from individual responsibility and the encouragement of prudent conduct, vital elements that the introduction of the state insurance scheme came to displace and destroy. In an analysis of friendly-society opposition to state insurance Green noted:

> The state could compel a man to contribute to state insurance but this would not make him careful or thrifty, or a good citizen. No less important, a state scheme would narrow the opportunities for people to acquire and employ the skills of self-organisation.[12]

In addition, the state was to usurp a natural and spontaneous predilection of people to save, and crowd out the mechanisms which were capable of providing a more efficient, competitive and individually tailored pension and benefit service. Some five million people have already voluntarily contracted out of the state earnings-related pension scheme since 1988. The growth of unit trusts and personal pensions over the past thirty years (on top of a huge investment by the personal sector in housing) is testimony to the voluntary savings impulse. In 1960 unit trust funds stood at £200 million. By 1994 the figure was almost £80 billion.

For personal pensions the growth has been even more dramatic: premiums paid in 1960 were £6 million. The figure now is more than £6 billion. Meanwhile the legacy of forty years of ballooning Beveridge has been a welfare system that is constantly under attack, and which has been the largest single contributor to the worst budget deficit in Britain's history and with vicious long-tail debt interest, rising by more than half to £26.5 billion in 1997-98.

What is clear is that resort to ever higher levels of tax does not solve the problem but places real constraints on the capacity of the economy to achieve longer-term and sustained recovery. The two tax-raising budgets have thus not lifted the burden but shifted it. No solution can be effective until the larger question behind the growth in the dependency machine is addressed: a redefinition of the functions of the British state: where it begins and where it ends, what it should provide and what it should best leave to others. Truly no domestic issue is now more important.

Notes

1. *Trends in Public Expenditure, 1987-89 to 1992-93*, Treasury Bulletin, Summer 1993, vol. 4, issue 2.

2. See Budget Statement and Red Book, March 1993.

3. Bill Robinson, *Financial Times*, August 17 1993.

4. Bill Robinson, *Financial Times*, August 10 1993.

5. To the author, April 1993.

6. Financial Statement and Budget Report, HM Treasury, November 1993.

7. *The Growth of Social Security*, DSS, 1993, p. 7.

8. Ibid., p. 8.

9. Ibid.

10. Richard Titmuss, *Problems of Social Policy*, HMSO and Longmans, Green, 1950, p. 506.

11. David Green, *Reinventing Civil Society: The Rediscovery of Welfare Without Politics*, Institute of Economic Affairs Health and Welfare Unit, 1993, p. 65.

12. Ibid., p. 53.

TABLE 11.1
SOCIAL SECURITY SPENDING (£m)

	1987-88	91-92	92-93	93-94	94-95	95-96
Total	49,145	69,048	78,343	84,495	88,250	92,650

Source: Department of Social Security.

TABLE 11.2
SPENDING ON GROUPS IN REAL TERMS (£m)

	1987-88	92-93	93-94	94-95	95-96
Elderly	31,920	34,480	35,200	34,750	35,450
Long-term sick	9,230	14,860	15,910	16,800	17,700
Short-term sick	1,480	1,160	1,170	1,200	1,200
Family	11,260	12,930	13,560	14,050	14,550
Unemployed	9,200	9,290	10,040	10,400	10,250
Widows and others	1,570	1,420	1,400	1,350	1,350
Total benefit spending	64,650	74,140	77,280	78,500	80,500

Source: Department of Social Security.

TABLE 11.3

THE DEPENDENCY BOOM

Estimated average numbers receiving benefits

	1992-93 thousands
Retirement pension	9,910
Widow's benefits	340
Unemployment benefit	715
Sickness benefit	135
Statutory sick pay	330
Invalidity benefit	1,490
Maternity allowance	15
Statutory maternity pay	85
Non-contributory retirement pension	30
War pension	310
Attendance allowance	765
Disability living allowance	935
Disability working allowance	5
Invalid care allowance	195
Severe disablement allowance	320
Industrial disablement benefit	295
Industrial death benefit	25
Income support	5,320
Child benefit	
numbers of children	12,485
numbers of families	6,895
One-parent benefit	895
Family credit	420
Housing benefit	
rent rebate	3,105
rent allowance	1,210
Community charge benefit	6,655

Source: Department of Social Security.

TABLE 11.4
GOVERNMENT SPENDING PLANS (£bn)

	1992-93	93-94	94-95	95-96	96-97	97-98
Control total	232.3	244.5	251.5	263.0	272.5	281
Cyclical social security	13.2	14.0	15.0	15.5	16.0	17.0
Central govnt. debt interest	17.4	19.5	22.5	24.5	25.5	26.5
Accounting adjustments	6.3	8.0	9.0	10.0	11.0	11.5
Total general government expenditure	269.2	286.0	297.5	313.0	325.0	336.0
Privatisation proceeds	8.1	5.5	5.5	1.0	1.0	1.0
Total general government expenditure	261.1	280.5	292.0	312.0	324.0	335.0

Source: Financial Statement and Budget Report 1994-94, HM
Treasury, November 1993.

TABLE 11.5
REAL GROWTH IN SOCIAL SECURITY BENEFIT
EXPENDITURE

	£ billion (1992/93 prices)					
	1949/50	59/60	69/70	79/80	89/90	92/93
Total expenditure	10.3	15.4	27.2	44.9	59.7	74.1
Index of expenditure in real terms (1949/50 = 100)	100	150	264	436	580	719
Expenditure as % of GDP	4.7	5.3	7.0	9.0	9.5	12.3

Source: Department of Social Security.

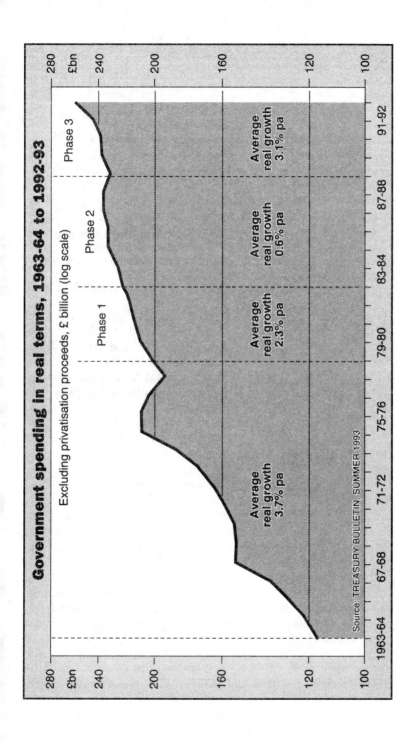

Government spending in real terms, 1963-64 to 1992-93

Excluding privatisation proceeds, £ billion (log scale)

Phase 1 — Average real growth 3.7% pa

Phase 1 — Average real growth 2.3% pa

Phase 2 — Average real growth 0.6% pa

Phase 3 — Average real growth 3.1% pa

Source: TREASURY BULLETIN, SUMMER 1993

1963-64   67-68   71-72   75-76   79-80   83-84   87-88   91-92

£bn   280   240   200   160   120   100

12

A New Agenda: Home Affairs

> We are therefore not authorised to abandon our country to its fate, or to act or advise as if it had no resource. There is no reason to apprehend, because ordinary means threaten to fail, that no others can spring up ... . The heart of the citizen is a perennial spring of energy to the state.
>
> Edmund Burke

By early 1994 Britain had arrived at a familiar conjunction of affairs: a country crying out for change and an elite bereft of ideas. Doubts about the calibre of Britain's leadership and her institutions were growing in scope and intensity. Beneath the daily crises that the government seemed to face could be detected a profound change of undercurrent, of a national tide that was on the turn, the vital pre-condition of impending change.

Giving a cutting edge to this mood of frustration was a sense of a government, not yet two years in office, that had lost direction and ideas: in almost every action it appeared vacuous and vapid. Its European policy was in tatters, its diversionary 'back to basics' rallying cry in disarray, the economy propelled by a problematic consumer-spending upturn and the Treasury too afraid to look forward and too ashamed to look back. What passed for ideas was a cacophony of empty slogans. What passed for a Cabinet was truly awful: headless chickens in outsize boots clanking dustbin lids.

The wider the gap between rhetoric and reality the greater the disillusion and the desire for change. This mood for change presents Britain with an epochal opportunity. One might fairly describe it as an imperative for change which needs to clear away the detritus of forty years. This necessary restoration and renewal depends on a fresh statement of pride, purpose, leadership and standards. Much of it will require an over-turn of the liberal orthodoxies that the political elite has championed for most of the post-war era. This change has to sweep through the education system, community institutions, the legal system, the courts and the corporate sector as well as government departments. The problem is not a lack of public acknowledgment of the need for change but a failure of the political class to respond. There is a sense of exhaustion, not only within government but across the political spectrum.

On the substantive areas of policy: the primacy of welfarism, the size and extent of government and Britain's integration with the EC, there has been a broad, all-party consensus. Voters have had no real choice, only frustration, on these issues. The official opposition has not only supported the growth of welfarism but has berated the government for not devoting more resource. Britain has now arrived at a position where, after four Conservative administrations committed to low taxation, the overall burden of tax is set to wipe out the Thatcher reductions.

What has thus become imperative is a fundamental re-thinking of the scope and functions of the state and the goals of economic policy. For few calls on British resource and resolve have been more burglar-like in their effect than the self-serving panaceas of successive governments over thirty years.

The reigning error in external relations has been the substitution of a regional view for a global vision with consequent loss of sovereignty, while on the domestic front it has been the substitution of welfare economics for the national interest with consequent loss of achievement. Government spending at £287 billion is now equivalent to £13 a day for every inhabitant of the UK and is approaching £20,000 a year for an average family with two children. The total under the government's control and excluding 'cyclical' social security, has risen 56 per cent in five years.

This spending, far from reviving the economy or resolving Britain's difficulties, has put enormous strain on the public finances and required huge tax increases. The recovery on which so much now rides needs to have an aim and purpose: a condition of sustained viability, both on the public finances and on the trade account. The one signal economic achievement of the early 1990s has been the fall in inflation, enabling interest rates to be lowered further after the initial reduction with Britain's expulsion from the ERM. But little fundamental thinking has been done on the nature of the recovery and what it is that this recovery should set out to achieve.

Britain, of course, cannot 'go it alone' to the extent that she may wish in matters of interest rate and fiscal policy given the consequences for the exchange rate. It is thus necessary for domestic priorities to change if Britain is not to lose control of interest and exchange rates. In particular the domestic economy has to be strengthened. Unemployment has fallen, but the calibre of new job creation, principally in the service sector, points to a continuing de-skilling of the employment base. Meanwhile a worryingly large number of young people are being marginalised or excluded from the formal economy altogether, with serious social implications.

Against this it may be argued that Britain is not suffering these problems in isolation. Balance of payments deficits, budget shortfalls and welfare spending pushed inexorably higher by demographics, have been outstanding features of almost all countries in the industrialised world and there seems nothing that Britain can do by itself to offset the *force majeure* of world economic conditions. It is thus argued that any improvement, other than competitive devaluation with its temporary boost to activity and employment, can only be brought about by a change in the international economy generally: the best excuse that can be thought of for doing nothing.

However, it is Britain's repeated failure to bear down on inflation that has led to exchange and interest-rate volatility and a marked vulnerability to external events and why, unless this syndrome is changed, external forces will become an increasingly painful and destabilising means of economic and social adjustment.

The rhetoric of Europe has masked the realities of Britain's economic interdependence with the rest of the world and the need for a transformation in attitudes to industry. Britain's need to transform her productive base, to build on its attractions relative to the continent and to continue to attract foreign direct investment critically depends on offering opportunities and conditions that are different from and better than those of her competitors. It requires a low tax and social wage-cost regime. The ability to take advantage of opportunities in changing international markets hinges both on expansion and qualitative improvement of the productive base. Without such a change Britain is destined to become a low-skill, low-investment, low-income tourist and service economy for the European mainland.

Policy-makers and commentators have despaired of how democratic countries can address the huge welfare and public expenditure commitments that have grown by virtue of the benefit culture that lies at the heart of the electoral process. Similar arguments were advanced in the mid-1970s that public-expenditure restraint, and in the late 1970s trade-union reform, were 'politically impossible'. Both were achieved (though the former was only of limited duration) because the consequences of not adapting were perceived by voters to be unacceptable. It may take a further budgetary crisis before the full truth of this position is understood. History teaches us that it is never too late, but it also teaches us that the price of delay keeps going up.

Little can come right until a reawakened confidence is in place. Such a consciousness is created less by exhortation than by example, and it is the first requirement of leadership that it sets an example. Yet the single most outstanding feature of British politics has been the collapse of vision and leadership and the paucity of outstanding leadership talent both across the government front bench and from the Opposition parties. To the extent that John Major's ill-fated call for 'back to basics' was simply another slogan seized upon for the momentary illusion of leadership, it reflected on the calibre of Major as Conservative leader and Prime Minister.

His accession to the premiership followed periods as Foreign Secretary and Chancellor so brief that it was impossible to form a view of his competence. Many government ministers now stay in jobs so fleetingly (Clarke had seven jobs in eleven years before becoming Chancellor) as to raise doubts about whether the positions they occupy have anything like the power and influence assumed.

The present culture and level of reward tends to draw many who have had little experience in spheres other than politics. Indeed it draws many who would otherwise fail or fall into obscurity. If a country continues to be led, not by winners but by unknowns, by the meretricious and by mediocrities, then a pervasive sense of lack of vision and decline should not surprise us.

Narrowness of vision is not confined to the political realm but is evident in critical areas of the business and corporate sector. A striking example is the electrical and defence electronics giant GEC. Notorious for maintaining a £2 billion cash pile during a period of unprecedented growth in electronics and telecommunications, shares in GEC underperformed the London stock market by 87 per cent between 1982 and 1991. Its major corporate move of recent years was the bitterly contested £2 billion take-over of rival Plessey in 1989. The rationale advanced at the time was that a mega-player was needed to win in European markets but, as Plessey's Sir John Clark warned, the rhetoric of Europe was a cloak behind which to 'take out' a competitor. The acquisition of Plessey failed to inject any new dynamism or to change the corporate culture of GEC. Group profits, stuck on a six-year plateau, simply moved to a higher one. Indeed retained profits in 1992 were lower than the level nine years before.

Britain has a strategic interest in building a presence in advanced electronics and telecommunications, the most lucrative and fastest-growing product areas in the industrialised world, offering outstanding rewards for product innovators and 'value-added' adaptation. Without growth by Britain's large corporations in this field the smaller satellites of suppliers and service companies have little by way of prospects. Yet GEC's recent capital spending has lagged lamentably: it has declined by more than 30 per cent since 1989 and is lacklustre by international comparison: the ratio of capital expenditure to turnover of 3.5 per cent is half that of Siemens.

Early in 1993 GEC failed to win a £1.2 billion order to supply radios for the army well into the next century – one of the largest defence electronics orders awarded this decade. Meanwhile it stood to lose on a £300 million order to design and develop radar for the European fighter aircraft because of a multi-million cost over-run. Power engineering group GEC Alsthom is the star division and has done well, but the group's failure to invest more boldly in its high-technology electronics expertise and instead retain a cash mountain must rank as the corporate lost opportunity of this generation.

In mitigation, it can be said that national failure to undertake major capital investment projects has been symptomatic of a corporate failure across all sectors of the economy and is the ultimate consequence of unprecedented inflation and monetary and interest-rate instability. For this reason, as much as management shortcoming, the characteristic feature of UK corporate development has been that of cutback, retrenchment, rationalisation and closure and a continuing switch to service-sector functions where the need for long-term capital expenditure is not as great and the return on capital quicker to show through.

It is no accident that many of the stock-market new issues in the early 1990s have been service-sector 'niche' companies whose activities bordered on the ephemeral and meretricious. Dreadnoughts are required, but instead stockbroker champagne is splashed on a flotilla made of matchsticks.

Price stability has to be regarded as one of the prime duties of the British state, on a par with defence and national security. It is vital for savers and investors. It is also the necessary foundation for competitive success. It is of critical importance in the financial sector and in particular banking and investment. Long-term lending and investment can only be made in a stable climate without the distorting effect of inflation on company trading performance, stock-market rating and balance-sheet ratios.

Such a climate, bringing with it low real as well as nominal interest rates, also enables major investment and infrastructure projects to be undertaken with greater confidence. The ability to plan ahead with confidence is critical. The cost of persistent inflation is particularly painful in recessions when companies find it difficult to continue to pay interest. Each one percentage point addition to the inflation rate is estimated to have added almost 6 per cent to the number of company insolvencies.[1] Above all, it will enable Britain to break free from the stop-go economics that has bedevilled major projects for the past thirty years and encouraged the banks and City institutions to opt for short-term returns.

The corrosive damage of inflation – and its persistence – has given rise to calls for an independent Bank of England with control over interest rates and monetary policy removed from political hands at the Treasury and placed with the Bank. But separating the operation of monetary from fiscal policy in this way runs the risk of a haphazard and accident-prone co-ordination of policy and, at worst, a war of attrition between the Bank and the legislature. As the recent history of the Bundesbank has shown, a central bank operating a tight monetary policy struggles to meet inflation targets when fiscal policy is loose and the government is incurring a large budget deficit.

The comparison drawn by advocates of a British independent central bank with the Bundesbank also fails to note the legitimacy attaching to the German central bank's operations and interest-rate decisions. This legitimacy derives both from the federal structure of the bank and the representative nature of its governing council comprised of senior banking officials drawn from the whole of Germany, and also from the widespread public aversion to inflation, rooted in the national memory of the Weimar Republic. The Bank of England enjoys no such status as it has no representative claim to authority and would not gain it simply by the legislative stroke of independence.

The Bank first needs to undertake a campaign on its own behalf to raise public understanding of its functions and its importance as a national institution. In the past it has spent too much time talking to the City and too little to the country as a whole. Its constituency is not sectional but national, yet it gives the appearance of not always recognising this fact. Its failure to develop a national base and the responsibility of educating the wider public on monetary policy is a key reason why inflation has been tolerated for so long. An independent central bank would be successful in sustaining low inflation only where there is widespread public recognition that price stability is less a 'policy' than one of the cornerstones of responsibility of the British state. Without such a cultural change, the Bank would soon find itself in conflict with an unreformed legislature on this fundamental issue, and with no certainty that it would prevail.

An equally potent change of culture is required on the public finances, both to effect a radical change in priorities and to make possible a sustained reduction in personal and corporate taxation to encourage the productive sector and attract foreign direct investment. The decision to address the budget deficit by tax increases rather than more widespread public expenditure reductions was an error of economic management by the government, setting aside the breach of its address to the voters as the party of low taxation.

At the start of the century the state consumed barely more than 10 per cent of the nation's wealth. The figure is now more than 45 per cent. The reason that public expenditure has climbed so rapidly is that the ratchet effect of long-term spending commitments makes it difficult to reduce spending during periods of economic boom.[2] When politically imperative bids force spending up in the following downturn the share of GDP taken by total public spending reaches a higher level than at the same point in the previous cycle. Conversely, when social-security spending eases during boom periods, other government projects rush in to take up the slack.

But when social security rises in recessions there is little or no reduction in other departments and so the 'planning total' rises. That is why the deterioration in the public finances is dramatically exposed in recessions but much of the damage is actually done in boom periods when the longer-term implications pass largely unnoticed.

Britain should aim not only for immediate reductions of significance, that is, at least £20 billion, but for a radical, long-term programme phased in over a generation to shift the bulk of provision into the private insurance sector, encourage the re-building of personal responsibility by tax reliefs and vouchers, dismantle the apparatus of multiple-claim dispensing, cut costs and sub-contract where applicable.

The biggest single problem within the public expenditure total is the growth in social security spending. There should be a phasing out of provision of universal benefits such as family and child benefits (saving £13.5 billion), curtailment of grants and hand-outs for single-parent families (now covering almost a million recipients), savings on unemployment benefits and savings in housing and community charge benefits.

The economist Barry Bracewell-Milnes, in a submission for the November 1993 budget, compiled a list of £100 billion of spending reductions and economies achievable over the next 25 years (see table 12.1 on pp. 173-4). Among other suggestions it included the phasing-out of mortgage-interest relief (saving £4 billion) with the added benefit of unwinding a long-term distortion in the savings market.

Accompanying the savings would be administrative reform within government and disengagement where appropriate. Of the £287 billion disbursed by the government, almost half involves collecting from one group and paying out to other groups – not always mutually exclusive. There should be greater privatisation and contracting out of services, reaching deep into general administration. For example, administrative costs of the Department of Social Security alone have swept from £2.4 billion in 1987-88 to £4.2 billion in 1993-94.

Almost ten million people are now in receipt of state retirement benefit costing £35.2 billion. There should be a long-term programme aiming to return retirement benefit to the private sector, with commensurate redirection in tax and national insurance contributions to approved private-sector schemes, leaving a safety net scheme in place. Health care should also be similarly privatised and contracted out. It is not the public sector's duty to provide services but to ensure that services are provided. Entitlement rather than provision should, say some, be the new catchphrase. But even this does not really go to the heart of the matter. It is not entitlement that should be encouraged but encouragement of self-provision. And that should extend to health care, pension benefits, unemployment insurance, personal-injury benefit and significant areas of education including pre-school nurseries and crêches.

The erosion of Britain's industrial base has carried serious economic and social consequences, a deterioration that could not have proceeded without an astonishing degree of complacency and self-delusion throughout the political and commercial establishment. In 1971, eight million people were employed in manufacturing and 11.6 million in services. In 1990 almost 16 million people were employed in services and only five million in manufacturing.

Throughout the 1980s there was a prevalent belief in government that the manufacturing sector did not matter, in the same way that a deficit in visible trade did not matter. These arguments were blind to certain salient features of the UK economy: that half of all consumer spending is on manufactured goods; that 70 per cent of exports of goods and services are accounted for by manufactures; that £7 billion of Corporation Tax is paid by manufacturing industry; and that, in addition to the five million jobs it directly provides, some five million are employed in supplying services to manufacturing.

Yet it is a sector that is operating well below potential, both in absolute and in relative terms. In the twenty years to 1990 manufacturing capacity rose by 20 per cent in Britain compared with 86 per cent in the United States and 129 per cent in Japan. As a result, not only does Britain's share of world trade suffer but her share of the home market is effectively surrendered. Between 1979 and 1991 manufacturing output rose by 6 per cent when household consumption climbed by 20 per cent, with an inevitable sharp rise in imported manufactured goods.

One of the most outstanding features of the past thirty years has been the surge in imports of manufactures. These increased their share of total imports from 5.1 per cent in 1955 to 35.6 per cent in 1980.

This was due in large part to the erosion of UK competitiveness during the 1970s but also to the switch in trade from the Commonwealth and emerging markets to the EC, in which the goods we imported were near-substitutes for our own exported manufactures. Foreign direct investment in the 1980s helped disguise the severity of the collapse of the manufacturing base under UK ownership and control. Welcome as such foreign investment has been, there are dangers in the loss of national control over key areas of manufacture. It should be encouraged as a supplement to, but not as a substitute for, enhancement of locally controlled capacity. It is less the loss of ownership and control of manufacturing plant *per se* that is problematic, so much as the consequent loss of top technical and decision-making personnel, research and development, finance and corporate advisory functions and local component supply and services which tend, over time, to be lost to the overseas parent or its agencies. BMW's acquisition of Rover in early 1994 aroused anxieties on this score.

Finally, while invisible earnings have made a huge contribution to the balance of payments, that contribution is notably volatile and is faced with intense international competition. In any event it is wrong to make a necessity out of the virtue of invisibles in this way and to neglect the requirement both on domestic economic grounds and the favourable balance of payments impact, of a healthy and vibrant productive base.

As a measure of the task to be achieved, the CBI has calculated that the UK needs an extra 1 per cent of world exports worth £10 billion a year and a drive towards import substitution to eliminate the trade deficit in manufactured goods. This is vital if industry is to break out of the trap that milch-cow politics and neglect has set for it: the highest returns are achieved by making products with a high technology or innovative cutting edge. These typically result from the highest standard of research and development. In sectors such as pharmaceuticals, research and development spending is markedly high, and product lead-times can be as long as eight to ten years. But the initial profit share in value-added can extend to 80 per cent to those who hold the patents. Those who get in first make the most money.

But British producers have been so engaged in fire-fighting and survival that long-term investment and research and development have suffered. Not enough has been ploughed back into the next generation of products. As a result, Britain has increasingly become a sub-assembly rather than an innovation-led economy with the associated loss of benefits. Meanwhile it should be the overall aim of fiscal policy to create and sustain one of the lowest tax regimes in the industrialised world. It should aim for a maximum rate of Corporation and personal income tax of 15 per cent and the abolition of taxes on saving, made possible by public-spending reductions and the removal of subsidies and allowances. The gains, measured by investment, inward capital flows, employment prospects and reward for enterprise, would be substantial.

As a major boost to London's position as a financial centre, consideration should be given to the introduction of bank secrecy protection for overseas depositors. It is the combination of low tax and bank secrecy that has historically accounted for the acknowledged success of Switzerland in this area. Britain has much to gain in an increasingly taxed and regulated world by helping the City of London to become not just the pre-eminent financial centre of Europe, but the pre-eminent off-shore financial centre for the world.

To this agenda other reforms can be added, such as further improvements in education and skills training, workfare schemes for unemployed school leavers, job re-training and other measures designed to help people out of the dependency trap. But all are essentially satellites moving around the imperative magnetic poles of sovereignty and viability.

It speaks volumes for Britain and the abdication of its governing elite that the stand-aside argument that 'government can do no more than create the environment in which the free market can operate' has allowed it to let the national interest slip through its fingers. It is telling that in the eleven years to 1991-92 while public expenditure on welfare and social security exploded, the areas to suffer the axe were trade, industry, energy and employment, whose share of government spending has almost halved to 2.9 per cent. Until these priorities are re-arranged, Britain will face accelerating decline with all that this implies for her economy, her society and her political institutions, and above all, the interests and security of her people. That decline is neither systemic nor inevitable, given a will to change and a wish to be back among the world's best.

Notes

1. See Bill Robinson, 'Soft heart of our problem', *Financial Times*, July 27 1993.

2. Wadhwani, 1985, cited by Dr Walter Eltis in the Esmée Fairbairn lecture 1992, 'The Financial Foundations of Industrial Success'.

TABLE 12.1
HOW TO CUT STATE SPENDING BY £100 BILLION*

Achievable over 25 years by structural reform in government, privatisation, contracting out, better targeting of benefits, cost efficiencies and economies.

item	saving (£bn)
General (all departments)	
Running costs, pay & manning levels	4.1
Sale of land, other	0.65
Social security	
Means testing non-contrib. benefits	1.0
Means testing invalidity benefit	2.0
Other economies	1.3
Structural reforms (i)	54.0
Health and personal social services	
Charges on medicines and savings	3.0
Structural changes (ii)	13.0

[continued overleaf]

item	saving (£bn)
Department of Education	
Fees and cost reductions	2.0
Savings through vouchers, etc.	13.0
Department of Trade & Industry	0.1
Department of Transport	
Road pricing, private funding	1.1
Common Agricultural Policy/EEC	0.45
Overseas Development Administration	0.35
Lord Chancellor's Department	0.55
Privatisation in police and fire	0.3
Local authorities	
Library fees, housing grant changes	0.8
Regional	1.25
Total	£99.95 billion

(i) Over the life of a generation, state support is confined to serious illness and disablement and the majority of caring done through family and personal contacts. Contributory benefits (currently £54 billion) fall by £42 billion as individuals switch to private insurance schemes and private provision. Cyclical social benefits are left at half their 1993-94 level, other benefits reduced to a tenth of current levels. Child benefit replaced by tax allowances; expenditure on non-contributory benefits falls from £20.7 billion to £11 billion. Residual social security spending at the end of the transitional period is estimated at £25 billion, or less than a third of its 1993-94 level.

(ii) Privatisation and switch to private insurance through enhanced and extended tax relief; charges for routine and minor treatment in 16-64 age group; savings in personal social services; overall savings of £16 billion on 1992-93 out-turn of £33.4 billion at the end of 25-year period, leaving £17 billion to be funded by the government.

* Compiled by Dr Barry Bracewell-Milnes, Economic Adviser, Institute of Directors.

Good Fences in Europe

After twenty-one years of EC membership, Britain's relationship with Europe has seldom been more problematic and the need for boldness never more certain. It is frequently asserted that there is nothing that Britain can do to halt the process of integration and that further loss of sovereignty and discretion is unavoidable. On the contrary: there is much that Britain can do, not only to assert her own interests but also to save Europe from being trapped in an economic twilight with the erosion in her world position matched only by the loss of democratic accountability of her institutions.

A fresh start by Britain on Europe is now long overdue. British policy on the EC is in disarray: the Major government cannot go forward on further integration because of public antipathy at home; it cannot go back because of commitments given in the signing of the Treaty on European Union.

The Prime Minister fought a prolonged and bruising battle to push the Maastricht Bill through Parliament. But barely a month after its ratification, with the ERM in tatters, he appeared anxious to distance himself from its central provisions on economic and monetary union, describing the insistence of European leaders' on adherence to the Treaty timetable as 'a rain dance'. Meanwhile Europe itself is split between those, like Delors, who have argued for the Treaty timetable to be maintained, and others, such as Bundesbank President Hans Tietmeyer, who regard it as hopelessly optimistic.

The continent is struggling to break out of a recession deeply exacerbated by the EC convergence programme and a high-interest-rate regime which has driven up unemployment. It is said that Britain, by 'going along' with integration, now has 'influence at the heart of Europe'. But attempts by Britain to speed recovery in Europe by pushing for labour market deregulation and a lowering of labour costs that have damaged competitiveness were swept to one side by Delors' grandiose plans

for huge infrastructure spending and 'telecommunications high-
ways' costing billions of ecus with an attendant scale of Europe-
wide borrowing that would push interest rates higher.

For British businessmen European integration has not developed at all in the way imagined when the Single Market
proposals were announced. Ambitious visions of cross-border
banking and financial mergers and alliances have simply not
materialised. Nor has there been anything like the scale of
cross-border merger and acquisition in the corporate sector. The
knitting together of economies through underlying convergence
has not occurred.

Britain's commercial, manufacturing and financial interests are keen to expand into a successful and prosperous
Europe and look to government to pursue these interests.
British companies want to take full advantage of continental
markets to locate plant in Europe, to make cross-border
acquisitions, forge joint ventures, build distribution networks
and enhance the Single Market to develop opportunities for
their goods and services.

What Britain and its business sector want are good trade and
financial relations with Europe. What Britain does not desire,
and believes to be deeply detrimental to the interests of Europe,
is a bureaucratic, centralised, socialist and uncompetitive trading bloc at the mercy of corporatist politicians who want to walk
tall in a grand supra-national federation.

What was looked for was a removal of barriers to trade. What
has actually transpired is a plethora of petty restrictions, harmonisation measures, costs and regulatory burdens and an
encroachment on sovereignty over which Britain and her people
now feel deep unease. There must now be a net retrieval of
self-government.

It is often asserted that Britain's problem with Europe
sprang from not joining the Common Market early enough. Yet
the problem is surely more fundamental: it is that she did not
undertake that overhaul and reconstruction that De Gaulle so
astutely divined, one that only the British people on their own
could undertake, and it is that overhaul and reconstruction that
has become imperative, and which her national interest now
requires her to undertake.

Not only has twenty-one years of EC membership failed to
obviate the need for that reconstruction but the reverse has been

the case. The increasing integration of the British economy and its governmental, administrative and legal systems with the EC, in particular the attempt at convergence through fixing of exchange rates, has been prejudicial to Britain's economy and threatens her global interests.

Post-Maastricht pressures have extended beyond the economic realm into proposals to absorb British foreign-policy-making and British interests into a collective European posture. But it is the increasing erosion of sovereignty in the fiscal and economic realm that has been particularly outstanding.

The loss of discretion is now an established fact in indirect taxation. Beginning with Article 99 of the Treaty of Rome which called for indirect taxation to be harmonised, and the adoption of VAT in 1967 (introduced in Britain three months after her accession in 1972) the EC has steadily encroached. In 1977 it laid down restrictions on what items member countries could exempt from VAT and required that VAT be levied on all other products. In 1988 Britain was required to introduce VAT on commercial fuel and power, water supply and building construction. In 1991 EC finance ministers adopted a standard rate of VAT of at least 15 per cent, a development that Britain, after initial deep reluctance, came to accept as legally binding. Once VAT is charged at 15 per cent it cannot subsequently be lowered or removed.

But it was the Treaty on European Union, the most significant constitutional change in Britain and on a par with the 1832 Reform Act and the 1689 Bill of Rights, that represented a quantum leap in the EC's discretion in UK affairs.

Whereas these previous milestones in British constitutional reform enhanced the legal and democratic rights of her citizens, Maastricht represents a huge reversal through the handing of power to tax, levy, fine and borrow to European commissioners, not one of them to be elected, and not one of them dismissable.

Article 99 gives the Council of Ministers authority to harmonise indirect taxation, sales taxes and excise duties; Article 100 gives the Council of Ministers power in the field of Single Market legislation; and Article 103 allows the Council to draft, by qualified majority voting, the broad guidelines of the economic policy of the member states.

Substantial power has been accorded to the European Central Bank. It will have authority to supervise all clearing banks and other financial institutions; the power to impose fines or sanctions on governments which fail to keep minimum reserves with the ECB and operate monetary policy along approved guidelines. Article 107 forbids individual country central banks such as the Bank of England from taking instructions from its government: these central banks become instead effective instruments of the ECB.

But the destruction of democratic accountability does not stop there. Britain has currently opted out of Stage Three of monetary union but will in due course come under strong pressure to conform, not least on the argument that once opted-in she will have a say in the running and operations of what will be the EC's most powerful institution in the economic realm.

Were Britain to do so she would find herself with two members in a central council of 28. The bank itself and the unelected European Commission will also have two seats apiece. So striking is the disregard for democratic accountability it is almost beyond belief that the leaders of Europe put their signatures to such a proposal. Tietmeyer has made clear his misgivings:

> An economic and currency union [would bring] with it such far-reaching transfers of sovereignty at Community level that the lack of democracy in the framework of the existing European institutions [could] no longer be accepted.[1]

As a priority Britain must first halt the subordination of Parliament and the institutions of the British state to the EC. The right of the British people to be protected by their sovereign democratic institutions is not for this generation, any more than it was for previous generations, voluntarily to dismantle.

Parliament must not just guard against any further encroachment on, but effect a restoration of, the primacy of the British Parliament, its financial institutions and its legal system. This requires action on three fronts. First would be a formal notice of Britain's withdrawal from Stage Two of economic and monetary union and resignation from the European Monetary Institute, together with all funding obligations pertaining to membership of the EMI. It is arguable whether Britain would not enjoy more influence as a free agent outside the EMI than as a 'tied agent' within. There is certainly no reason to believe the tired Foreign Office assertion that by 'going along' with participation Britain would enjoy any more 'influence' than has accrued to her by virtue of previous surrenders of sovereignty.

In opting out of Stage Two of economic and monetary union Britain still has an obligation to pursue interest and exchange-rate policies compatible with orderly markets and stability, and to mitigate exchange-rate volatility by informal co-operation and liaison between central banks.

It is argued, notably by the distinguished *Financial Times* commentator Sir Sam Brittan,[2] that Britain cannot fully control inflation on her own, however rigorous domestic monetary policy may be, but needs to take part in international co-ordination through a mechanism such as the EMI. Equally there are benefits to be gained by practical measures to minimise exchange-rate volatility.

But it is one thing to work constructively to smooth day-to-day operations in the markets. It is another to become drawn into some vast edifice of monetary and political union. The EMI has been founded to serve a greater purpose and agenda than minimising exchange-rate turbulence. As the forerunner of the ECB it is an essential cog in the wheel of monetary and political union. It is not necessary for the UK, in coming to practical arrangements over her trade, interest-rate and exchange-rate policy, to surrender the sovereignty of her domestic institutions and legal system. Canada, one of the Group of Seven leading industrial nations, has not found it a requirement of her economic well-being to enter into economic and political union with the United States. Yet so intense is the ambition to impose this agenda on Europe that Delors proposed controls on the movement of capital traffic to prevent future speculative attacks on the ERM. As Tietmeyer pointed out:

> Free capital traffic is a necessary corollary to a free exchange of goods and services. It is in addition to that a vital condition for the optimal use of capital.[3]

As a first step, Britain should not be afraid to espouse, and act as a catalyst for, a 'multi-speed' EC, allowing for differences and divergencies in the underlying economies. Better relations between the states of Europe will be achieved by encouraging areas of policy discretion in which they can make their own decisions rather than through an elaborate system of regulation and intervention. Ironically, the creation of such a system is more likely to act as a transmitter of German hegemony than as a brake on it.

Countries should be free to merge their economies and currencies, should they mutually wish to, while respecting the right of other EC countries to pursue convergence at their own speed or, for that matter, the right not to converge at all. In this role Britain would only be creating a welcome and overdue recognition that monetary and political union can in any event only be advanced by a convergence of the underlying economies, a process that must of necessity take time, and that cannot be accelerated by political fiat.

Secondly, Britain should halt any further incursion of Community law into the United Kingdom, her vulnerability to this encroachment being greater than that of other member states by virtue of not having, as they do, a written constitution. This brake on encroachment can be effected by amendment of sections two and three of the European Communities Act (3) so as to bring about:

(1) A recognition of the ultimate supremacy of Parliament over all Community law, with the right to revoke in whole or in part, or vary the operation of, Community law, spelt out and legally recognised.

(2) An express list of 'reserved' or ring-fenced matters which no Community law should be allowed to affect, including, *inter alia*, the constitution and procedure of Parliament and election to it; the relationship between government, Parliament and the courts; and United Kingdom defence and security matters. (Such a list of areas to be ring-fenced was secretly drawn up during the final year of Mrs Thatcher's tenure as Prime Minister.)

(3) An appeals procedure under which conflicts between Acts of Parliament and Community law can be referred to the Lord President who would propose Parliamentary orders where appropriate.

(4) Reserve powers to nullify decisions or acts of Community institutions so that they have no effect under the laws of the

United Kingdom (thus preventing, for example, the Social Chapter by the 'back door').

(5) Withdrawal of endorsement of the doctrine of 'occupied field' or *'acquis communautaire'* under which the accretion of legal rights by the institutions of the EC is held to be permanent and irreversible.[4]

Thirdly, Britain should cap her contributions to the EC budget pending reform of the Common Agricultural Policy. It is wasteful, inefficient and a huge cost on consumers. Britain joined the EC, not in order to dismantle national sovereignty throughout Europe, but to promote and expand free trade in goods and services. To assist in the growth of the European Single Market Britain should press for reductions in government subsidies to state industries on the Continent. She should also repudiate the system of Community-directed social funds and regional 'infrastructure' subventions which are little more than a return to the central planning and direction of economies that collapsed so spectacularly in the former Soviet Union. Precedent for such action in defence of essential national interests can be found in the policy of non-co-operation adopted by President De Gaulle in 1965.

In the event of the Community preventing Britain from acting in the defence of her essential national interests Britain should consider replacing her formal membership of the EC in favour of affiliate status, with a system of bilateral trade and finance agreements similar to those in force between Switzerland and the EC. (It is noteworthy that, far from atrophying by being outside the EC, the Swiss financial sector has continued to flourish and leading banks such as Swiss Bank Corporation and UBS have become successful global companies.) There is, of course, the ultimate sanction of non-payment of contributions to the EC budget, the spectre of which was deployed during the renegotiation of Britain's budget contribution in the early 1980s. As Britain is the second largest net contributor to the budget, this is not a step to be taken lightly, or indeed, from the Community's view, to be provoked where it can be avoided.

In a world of huge and increasing cross-border capital flows and globalisation of trade and investment it is folly to imagine a policy of isolationism in trade, even if desired. It is not just that Britain positively wishes to be part of this global market:

the world has moved on and the world outside Europe is beckoning. Nor is there any desire on a political level but for the most cordial relations with Europe. Assertion by Britain of the desire to be sovereign in her domestic affairs, or of having trading interests and arrangements with other countries, should no more make for poor relations with Europe than, say, the acceptance of the fact of independence now enjoyed by the countries of central Europe should prevent cordial trade and diplomatic relations with Russia.

There is nothing about interdependence in trade and finance *per se* that requires countries and peoples to conform in their internal political and domestic social affairs. But there is benefit in mindfulness and respect for what makes us culturally and politically separate as much as what draws us near. The poet Robert Frost put it well: 'Good fences make good neighbours.'

Notes

1. Hans Tietmeyer, 'Les Echos' Conference, Paris, October 15 1993.
2. Sam Britain, 'Why we cannot just "go it alone" ', *Financial Times*, November 11 1993.
3. Tietmeyer, loc. cit.
4. See Martin Howe, *Europe and the Constitution after Maastricht*, 1992, which sets out a programme of constitutional safeguards in some detail.

Britain or Benelux West?

A public swimming pool in Cornwall, an industrial clearance project in the Midlands, a road extension in the Scottish highlands – throughout Britain dozens of environmental and worthy public projects sport the blue EC flag with its circle of gold stars. The signboards proclaim: 'Another project funded by EC regional funds.'

What is it we feel as we drive by? A rush of gratitude to Jacques Delors? Irritation at this gratuitous proselytising by Brussels? Annoyance that it is British taxpayers' money behind the EC's munificence?

The signs are meant to counter the negative image of the EC and to encourage a perception of Britain as a Euro-beneficiary: the recipient of generous regional infrastructure funds. What they are designed to elicit is gratitude. What they provoke is disquiet. They suggest a home economy too weak to look after itself, a Big Brother paternalism accompanied by a sense of dependence. What local authority or government department would not willingly reach out its hand for more, or suppress a view that may be critical for fear of missing out in the next round of project applications?

Disbursements of regional and social funds – Britain received almost £1 billion in 1992 although her net contribution to the EC budget overall was more than £2 billion – have a huge propaganda value for the EC. They have had minimal effect in their aim of raising economic performance in the poorer regions. But they are the most outward and visible symbol of the EC 'ideal' at work.

It is this arm of the Community that Delors has set out to enlarge dramatically: a 150 billion ecu (£110 billion) spending programme over five years on telecommunications networks; 250 billion ecu (£185 billion) by the end of the decade on transport and energy (55,000 kilometres of road); 174 billion ecu

(£128 billion) on environmental projects including cleaning up the Mediterranean and the Baltic.

The vast ambition of Delors suggests not so much the mind of a French corporatist as of a modern-day Metternich: the whole of the continent is to be one huge civil engineering and construction park, filled with the noise of infrastructure projects, panoramic environmental improvement and army-size job-creation schemes.

Political pressure for these projects is set to intensify, both as a means of accelerating recovery on the continent and revitalising the drive for union. For Britain they represent a deepening of her dilemma: an intuitive reluctance to give support and encouragement on the grounds of the tax, borrowing and interest-rate implications; but an equal desire not to prejudice her prospects of securing a share of the spoils.

It is the EC ratchet in another form: however much Britain may wish to slow down or halt the power of EC institutions and the move to federal union, she finds herself up against a tireless and unstoppable machine. From the beginning this momentum for integration has been like a bicycle: if it is not moving forward it falls down. This momentum, is if anything, strengthened by the EC's failure in the economic realm: it feeds as much on setback as on advance. In doing so, it presents Britain with an intensifying test of her European commitment. She will be continually forced to choose, not so much between whether to go along or not to go along as how far she can comply without incurring further antipathy at home.

The danger is that no clear decision will be made: Britain will continue to be swept down the Euro-stream at increasing speed, making a virtue of her ambiguity and holding a reluctant parliament together by fudge and indecision. Moreover, in the absence of a firm resolution to draw a line on further encroachment, the pull of accelerating convergence will prevail whether her domestic economy prospers or declines. For example, under a 'high road' scenario in which low inflation and interest rates are maintained and the economy continues to recover, sterling would continue to make good her post-September 1992 fall against the Deutschemark. Pressure from the Treasury to 'lock in the gains' by membership of a reformulated European exchange-rate mechanism would be augmented by keen continental desire to prevent Britain from again taking advantage (as

Europeans see it) of structural weakness in her economy by competitive devaluation. By the end of the decade the traumas of 1992 will have been long forgotten, the landscape will have changed and Britain will be a full member of the European currency system with the grounds for continuing the opt-out from Stage Three of full union no longer seen as valid or appropriate.

Under the 'low road' scenario the outcome would be the same. It would go something like this. The economy hits capacity constraints, imports rise as a consumer boom continues unchecked, with a consequent impact on the balance of payments. Concern over the sustainability of growth is compounded by political uncertanties following the downfall of the Major government and the failure of the opposition to secure an overall majority. Fundamental and long-standing problems in the economy go unaddressed as the country enters a period of political turbulence. Pressure builds on the currency, resulting in a depreciation against the Deutschemark and consequent worries about a rekindling of inflation. Meanwhile, government spending is increased to finance an ambitious programme of infrastructure renewal, augmented by an application for support from the European regional fund.

As cost pressures arising from sterling's weakness both against the dollar and the leading European currencies work through to industry, a series of minority administrations and coalitions unsuccessfully seek to implement pay and price controls. Inflation continues to rise and there are further and increasingly severe speculative attacks on the currency. As sterling continues to weaken, appeals are lodged with the European Court of Justice that Britain is operating an exchange-rate policy in breach of her obligations to the common interests of the Community. Britain then seeks a multi-billion dollar international loan to support the pound. A pre-condition of EC-member-country support – and further regional-fund support – is that Britain agrees to closer EC monitoring of her economy and to opt in to Stage Three of economic and monetary union.

Meanwhile, whichever way the scenario unfolds, Europe itself is not standing still. The convergence agenda would take a quantum leap forward with the adoption of a programme to tackle Eurosclerosis via the Delors route of hugely enhanced regional-fund and infrastructure spending. These in time would take on the status and character of structural adjustment programmes, financed by a combination of EC grants and loans. To the extent that regional fund enlargement was justified on the grounds that it would help accelerate convergence of the underlying economies, Britain would find it difficult to oppose as she has repeatedly emphasised the importance of such underlying convergence before further steps are taken down the road of monetary union.

This process would also intensify calls for greater segmentation of the EC economy and geographic specialisation if duplication and waste of resources are to be avoided. It would be absurd, for example, if member states sought to secure finance to augment their market share of, say, telecommunications or automotive assembly when such gain would be at the expense of operations in another EC member state.

EC-wide economic planning and control would become increasingly more detailed and rigorous: certain industries would be designated for certain countries and each country would develop sector specialisms. Once the EC goes down the 'structural adjustment' route, particularly on any enlargement of membership, the mechanics of planning and co-ordination grow exponentially: the process becomes highly centralised and bureaucratic.

Such programmes would galvanise political integration, not only by whetting appetites for substantial enlargement of the Community's resources for regional funds but also for the agencies of disbursement. The bigger the disbursements from the centre the stronger the demands for representation and for accountability.

The European Parliament would become the forum for expenditure appeals, giving legitimacy to European Commission pressure on member countries for greater revenue-raising powers, more 'resources', more staff. The resulting growth of the central bureaucracy alone would be formidable. The magnitude and complexity of the technology required for the functioning of the European Parliament is already breathtaking before any further enlargement is allowed for. Some 10,000 Community meetings have to be interpreted in nine official languages, requiring 72 combinations for interpreting purposes. The use of 16 languages as formally envisaged will result in 240 combinations requiring 54 interpreters for one meeting of a single committee.

Enlargement of the scope, powers and functions of the European Parliament is a process that Britain, together with several other member states, has viewed with misgiving and disquiet. But over the next decade an expansion seem unavoidable. Yet already Brussels is coming to resemble the Hapsburg empire in its worst features – bureaucratic in-fighting, corruption, dozens of political parties, log-rolling alliances, regional cabals and splinter groups, competing for the political rewards that come with the disbursement of money, power and patronage. By the end the Hapsburg rule could only be maintained by bureaucrats: it took 25 signatories to validate a tax payment. One in four people worked for the state.

As much for self-interest as for administrative workability, geographic groupings and clusters are likely to emerge to represent the interests of the region against the centralising pull of the Franco-German axis: the Scandanavian countries advancing their claims against those of the Mediterranean bloc; the Benelux countries and Britain seeking to ensure that disbursements are not a one-way flow from industrial economies to agrarian, or effective rewards for failure and under-performance. On this scenario Benelux West is no flight of fancy but a regional administrative statement of the destiny that awaits Britain in a federal Europe. Yet how far and how fast the EC can build up infrastructure and regional spending will hinge on the strength of perceived common interest, and there is no widespread perception in Britain that regional spending in, say, Greece will be of indirect benefit to the whole.

One means of mitigating a latter-day Balkanisation of Europe is through expansion, which would loosen the centralising pull. But there is no agreement within the EC as to what its natural or political boundaries are, what is 'European' and what is not. And this question of boundary goes to the heart of a fundamental problem at the EC. For if it cannot agree on its boundaries and on its definition, where it begins and where it ends, who is 'European' and who is not, how much more difficult it is going to be to secure agreement on a common currency, a common parliament and a common bank. One group within the EC, including Britain, would prefer to see a widening of membership to embrace the central European states of Poland, Hungary, the Czech Lands and Slovakia, while another wishes to press ahead with a deepening of the union. It is a divide that will constantly recur, with no certainty that it will be resolved. Indeed, plans to widen the EC to include Austria, Sweden, Finland and Norway have proved fraught with problems. Enlargement sparked huge controversy over the procedure for voting in the Council of Ministers, in particular changes in the number of votes required to block EC legislation. Britain opposed the changes on the grounds that they would weaken her power of veto. Under the proposed system 250 million Europeans could be outvoted by 120 million. Enlargement negotiations also brought a scramble among the newcomers for EC handouts, with the result that the net cost of their membership is expected to total almost £3 billion in the first four years.

Meanwhile, is it inevitable that Britain will go down the road to Benelux West? The greatest impetus would come from any further economic setback which would render her more vulnerable to monitoring and control by EC institutions as a precondition for assistance. But there is nothing 'inevitable' about such a decline. Those who bewail Britain's inability to stand apart from continental political integration overlook that since 1992 she has demonstrated an ability to sustain low inflation and secure – alone among EC countries in 1993 – an economic recovery. Outside Europe the stimulus is being given to the global economy by the emerging market economies of Asia, the Pacific Rim and Latin America. Not only does Britain have substantial portfolio investments in these areas but her leading companies are now setting up manufacturing plant or building distribution networks for the sale of British goods and services. Britain has also proved highly successful in the financial services field covering equity and bond-market transactions, asset management, portfolio services, corporate finance and insurance: 'invisible earnings' which are fast expanding.

A further strength has been her success in attracting direct investment from overseas, being the favoured choice not only of American and Japanese companies, but also those of EC member countries. This is a reflection of her success in improving productivity and competitiveness following labour market deregulation in the 1980s. That there is much to be done to enhance the productive base is evident. But there are as much grounds for hope as there are areas to improve.

There is nothing in Britain's disposition that suggests that European integration is a compelling necessity. Here are tremendous strengths, and the greatest of these are to be found in her culture and her institutions, which rank among the best in the world. The mood of self-doubt and angst that has spread throughout Britain in the 1990s is not so much because her institutions *per se* have been found wanting, as because their leadership has. Britain despairs, not of her Parliament, but of those who run it; not of her parties, but of the lack of vision of their leaders; not of her legal system, but of the inconsistency of their judges; not of her church, but of the secularity of its ministers.

As for her 57 million citizens, there can be found all manner of imperfections and a perennial spring of hope. Being written off as beyond hope has become a condition of Britishness. It was not some frivolous whim that caused Edmund Burke to advise that 'the public must never be regarded as incurable'. The British spirit was seldom lower than at the beginning of the Seven Years War, and when theories of the innate feebleness of the British character had become best-sellers of the time.

But as Burke reminded us, while our leaders were prepared to abandon us 'to a direct confession of our inferiority to France, and whilst many, very many, were ready to act upon a sense of that inferiority, a few months effected a total change in our variable minds. We emerged from the gulf of that speculative despondency and were buoyed up to the highest point of practical vigour.'[1] Never say the die is cast for the British people.

Note

1. *Selections from the Speeches and Writings of Edmund Burke*, George Routledge & Sons, n.d., p. 367.

Bibliography

Atkinson, Rodney, *Your Country, Your Democracy*, Campaign for an Independent Britain, 1991.

Banque Paribas, 'Maastricht, The State of the Union', in *Conjuncture*, April 1993.

Baring Securities, 'Asia's Dragons and Mini Dragons', *Quarterly Economic Review*, 1993.

Blake, Robert, *The Decline of Power, 1915-1964*, Granada, 1985.

Blakey, George, *A Post-war History of the London Stock Market, 1945-1992*, Mercury, 1993.

Bracewell-Milnes, Barry, *Customers Back in Charge: A Charter for Government Spending*, Institute of Directors, 1993.

Brown, William, *Europe and the Convergence Agenda*, J.P. Morgan, November 1992.

Browning, Peter, *The Treasury and Economic Policy 1964-1985*, Longman, 1986.

Bruges Group, *The Erosion of Democracy*, Ferguson, Minogue and Regan, introduction by Martin Holmes, Occasional Paper no. 14, 1993.

Bundesbank, *The Deutsche Bundesbank and its Functions*, Bundesbank, 1989.

Burk, Kathleen & Cairncross, Alec, *'Goodbye, Great Britain': The 1976 IMF Crisis*, Yale University Press, 1992.

Burkitt, B., Baimbridge, M. & Reed, S., *From Rome to Maastricht: A reappraisal of Britain's Membership of the European Community*, Campaign for an Independent Britain, 1992.

Bush, Stephen & Gill, *Britain's Future: The Meaning of the Maastricht Treaty*, Prosyma Research, 1992.

Cain, P.J. & Hopkins, A.G., *British Imperialism*, vol.I *Innovation and Expansion*, vol. II *Crisis and Deconstruction*, Longman, 1993.

Cairncross, Alec, *The British Economy since 1945*, Blackwell, 1992.

Cairncross, Frances & Alec, *The Legacy of the Golden Age: The 1960s and their Economic Consequences*, Routledge, 1992.

Capel, James, *European Recession – How Long and How Deep?* Economic research paper, March 1993.

Capel, James, *Global Economics Monthly*, 1993

Cash, William, *Against a Federal Europe: The Battle for Britain*, Duckworth, 1991.

Cash, William, *Europe: The Crunch*, Duckworth, 1992.

Childs, David, *Britain Since 1945: A Political History*, Routledge, 1992.

Eltis, Walter, *Classical Economics, Public Expenditure and Growth*, Edward Elgar, 1993.

Europe's Constitutional Future, IEA Readings, Institute of Economic Affairs, 1990.

Evans, Douglas, *While Britain Slept: The Selling of the Common Market*, Gollancz, 1975.

Financial Statement and Budget Report, 1993-1994 & 1994-1995. HM Treasury.

George, Stephen, *Britain and European Integration Since 1945*, Institute of Contemporary British History, Blackwell, 1991.

Green, David, *Reinventing Civil Society: The Rediscovery of Welfare Without Politics*, IEA Health and Welfare Unit, Choice in Welfare Series no. 17, 1993.

Hill, Stephen, *Lions Led by Donkeys: How to Make the Real Economy Work*, Duckworth, 1992.

Hill, Stephen (ed.) *Visions of Europe*, Duckworth, 1993.

Holmes, Martin, *Beyond Europe: Selected Essays 1989-1993*, Nelson & Pollard Publishing, 1993.

Howe, Martin, *Europe and the Constitution after Maastricht*, Nelson & Pollard, Oxford 1992.

Howell, Michael, & Cozzini, Angela, *Cross Border Capital Flows*, Baring Securities, 1993.

Huhne, Christopher, *Real World Economics*, Penguin, 1991.

Johnson, Christopher, *The Economy under Mrs Thatcher, 1979-1990*, Penguin, 1991.

Johnson, Paul, *The Offshore Islanders: A History of the English People*, Weidenfeld & Nicolson, 1972.

King, Mervyn, *The Bundesbank: A view from the Bank of England*, Bank of England, May 1993.

Keegan, William, *The Spectre of Capitalism*, Radius, 1992.

Lawson, Nigel, *The View from No. 11: Memoirs of a Tory Radical*, Bantam Press, 1992.

Marten, Neil, *The Common Market, No Middle Way*, Common Market Safeguards Campaign, 1974.

Martin, Bill, *Beyond Our Ken*, UBS, 1993.

Minford, Patrick, (ed.), *The Cost of Europe*, Manchester University Press, 1992.

Nolling, Wilhelm, *Monetary Policy in Europe after Maastricht*, St. Martin's Press, 1993.

Pimlott, Ben, *Harold Wilson*, Harper Collins, 1993.

Pollard, Sidney, *The Development of the British Economy, 1914-1980*.

Powell, Enoch, *Nation or No Nation: Six Years in British Politics*, ed. Richard Ritchie, B.T. Batsford, 1978.

Powell, Enoch, *On 1992*, ed. Richard Ritchie, Anaya Publishers, 1989.

Pratten, Cliff, *Overseas Investments, Capital Gains and the Balance of Payments*, Institute of Economic Affairs, Research Monograph no. 48, 1992.

Prest & Coppock, *UK Economy: A Manual of Applied Economics*, Weidenfeld and Nicolson, 1980.

Reading, Brian, 'The Great World Boom 1993-2013', in *Britain & Overseas*, 1993.

Reynolds, David, *Britannia Overruled: British Policy & World Power in the 20th Century*, Longman, 1991.

Ridley, Nicholas, *'My Style of Government': The Thatcher Years*, Hutchinson, 1991.

Robbins, Keith, *The Eclipse of a Great Power: Modern Britain 1870-1975*, Longman, 1983.

Roberts, Richard, *Schroders: Merchants & Bankers*, Macmillan, 1992.

Roche, David, *China!* Report on the Morgan Stanley tour of China, Morgan Stanley International Investment Research, 1993.

Roche, David, *Restructuring and the Unbearable Process of European Disintegration*, Morgan Stanley International Investment Research, May 1993.

Schmieding, Holger, *The End of the German Miracle? Germany's Economic Prospects in Historical Perspective*, Merrill Lynch, December 1992.

Sked, Alan, *Good Europeans*, Bruges Group Occasional Paper no. 4, 1989.

Sked, Alan, *Time for Principle*, Bruges Group, 1992.

Skidelsky, R.J.A., *Interests & Obsessions: Historical Essays*, Macmillan, 1993.

Smith, David, *From Boom to Bust: Trial and Error in British Economic Policy*, Penguin, 1992.

Social Security, Departmental Report, Department of Social Security, 1993.

Spicer, Michael, *A Treaty Too Far: A New Policy for Europe*, Fourth Estate, 1992.

Stock Exchange Quarterly and *Quality of Markets Review*, Stock Exchange, July-September 1993.

Thatcher, Margaret, *The Downing Street Years*, Harper Collins, 1993.

Walters, *Sterling in Danger*, 1990.

Ziegler, Philip, *The Sixth Great Power: Barings, 1762-1929*, Collins, 1988.

Index